Ensuring Civility Online

Ensuring Civility Online

Professional Etiquette in the Virtual Workplace

Virginia Hemby

BEP

BUSINESS EXPERT PRESS

Leader in applied, concise business books

Ensuring Civility Online: Professional Etiquette in the Virtual Workplace

Copyright © Business Expert Press, LLC, 2024

Cover design by Charlene Kronstedt

Interior design by Exeter Premedia Services Private Ltd., Chennai, India

First published in 2023 by
Business Expert Press, LLC
222 East 46th Street, New York, NY 10017
www.businessexpertpress.com

ISBN-13: 978-1-63742-543-5 (paperback)
ISBN-13: 978-1-63742-544-2 (e-book)

Business Expert Press Corporate Communication Collection

First edition: 2023

10 9 8 7 6 5 4 3 2 1

Description

In a world of increasing self-expression and self-promotion, the practice of etiquette seems absent in many everyday encounters. Additionally, the constant connectivity offered by technology has led to a decline in interpersonal communication skills, including empathy, civility, and common courtesy.

Despite the fact that technology has allowed for, and even promoted, the widespread growth of incivility, the main culprit behind rudeness remains human behavior. While numerous books about incivility are available, the focus of those publications is most often on the topic of incivility and not on the means to reduce or alleviate its presence.

Ensuring Civility Online: Professional Etiquette in the Virtual Workplace provides a practical approach with clear guidelines for managing behavior in a virtual environment. The concise content will be helpful to trainers, educators, managers, employees, students, conference planners, conference attendees, and any others attempting to navigate the virtual environment in a professional manner. This book will provide you with the knowledge and tools needed to conduct yourself professionally in any virtual setting.

Keywords

virtual environment; civility; rules for online behavior; etiquette; workplace protocol; e-mail introductions; polite conversation; meetings; interviews; cyberbullying; digital etiquette; incivility; professional image/ personal image; social media; texting; virtual learning; online meetings

Contents

Testimonials

"Ensuring Civility Online: Professional Etiquette in the Virtual Workplace *is a must read for everyone who desires to make a good impression when communicating online. With the many online meetings as well as online communication platforms being used by business professionals today, it is of vital importance to know how to communicate professionally.*

In addition to technology, the virtual workplace has a role to play in some of the incivility being found in today's environment. The book does an excellent job explaining reasons behind some of the incivility that appears frequently in online and virtual environments. Dr. Hemby includes important data and facts from other credible sources to support what she is recommending.

The book is easy to read and full of real examples of poor communication to prove how often poor etiquette is practiced. Although people may be communicating in a very uncivil manner, they may not even realize the impression they are making on those with whom they are communicating. The checklists included in the book provide an easy-to-use list of rules and/or guidelines to follow in e-mail, instant messaging, social media, text messaging, online classes, training sessions, meetings, and presentations. These checklists provide an easy way to provide new information and reminders about best practices of communication.

The book would provide valuable information to students in business communication type classes at the undergraduate and/or graduate level. Business professionals and trainers also could benefit from the information provided in the book. The book discusses and gives examples of both active and passive incivility. As Dr. Hemby said, "incivility did not begin with the growth in technology," but technology has led to some of the forms of incivility now being identified in the world of business. Dr. Hemby provides some of the history behind incivility so that the reader can see that it is not a new problem. Instead, the reader can see that incivility is a continuing problem that needs to be addressed and resolved.

As Dr. Hemby said, a "suggested method for managing incivility is the development and implementation of a policy and code of conduct in the workplace directed toward encouraging respect and acceptable behaviors." This book could help provide the framework for such a policy and code of conduct. The book also includes good references for those who wish to continue to learn more about the topic.

Dr. Hemby suggests that "organizations in which leaders display the behaviors desired of employees and embody the principals of respect and courtesy, stand a greater chance of reducing incidences of incivility than do others." Her book can help leaders better understand the importance of civility in communication and can also help leaders to monitor and maybe improve their own communication.

In conclusion, I recommend everyone wishing to make a good impression on those with whom they interact in online and virtual environments read Ensuring Civility Online: Professional Etiquette in the Virtual Workplace."
—Dr. Barbara Hagler, Professor Emerita, Workforce Education and Development, Southern Illinois University, Carbondale, Illinois

"Ensuring Civility Online: Professional Etiquette in the Virtual Workplace *is a good book addressing civility and professional etiquette through technology and in the workplace. The content is easy to comprehend. I consider the book a good foundation for organizations to reference when needing an understanding of civility as well as adhering to when faced with issues of incivility and unprofessional etiquette.*

The author has done a remarkable job researching and applying the topic to the 21st-century workplace."—**Dr. Raholanda White, Professor, Department of Marketing, Middle Tennessee State University, Murfreesboro, Tennessee**

"I enjoyed reading Ensuring Civility Online: Professional Etiquette in the Virtual Workplace. *I found it to be well-written, well-researched, and quite informative. I believe this book should be mandatory reading for business CEOs, all business students, and, in particular, any individual who seeks to communicate effectively and courteously with their broad consumer base."*
—Dr. Robert E. Grubb, Retired, Criminal Justice Professor, Johnson City, TN

Acknowledgments

Thank you to my family for always being understanding of the time I devote to my projects. You never complain, and for that, I am beyond grateful.

This book is dedicated to my wonderful dad, James Hemby, who left us in May 2022. His unending faith in my abilities and his belief that I could conquer the world shaped me into the person I am. I miss his smile and our visits while sitting in the rocking chairs on the front porch. I now understand why you always taught me to be strong. You knew that one day, I would need that strength to bear your loss.

Introduction

Several years into my teaching career and well into the development and deployment of online courses, I decided to try something different and offer my students an opportunity to evaluate my classes via the use of a nonstandardized method, one often found in restaurants and other establishments: the anonymous Suggestion Box. While I appreciated the student evaluation instrument in use by the university, I felt it fell short of providing the type of information that instructors could really use. It merely asked students to complete a Likert-scale instrument that included no open-ended questions that allowed for or encouraged feedback to explain or support their selection of responses for any statements on the evaluation. While numbers are important, they do not ultimately reveal the reasons behind choices on a Likert-scale questionnaire.

Previously, I had been employed at an institution in another state where the student evaluation instrument had included open-ended questions that specifically sought to delve into reasons why students rated an instructor or a course in a specific manner. For example, one of the questions asked, "What did you like best about this course?" In reviewing the results of my students' evaluations, I always skimmed the *numbers* section and went straight to the open-ended responses. I learned more from my students by reading their comments than I ever would learn by simply reviewing the scores from the total student evaluation. I appreciated their comments and quite often made changes to my courses based on their suggestions. Obviously, as in any statistical analyses, I would find what we term *outliers*—and the open-ended question responses were no different as I would find the "I hated this course," "I hated this professor," type responses—no constructive feedback, just a mechanism for getting one last zinger at the course instructor. I mentally removed those outliers from the list and reviewed the constructive comments that offered me insight into the students' ways of thinking and their suggestions for improvements to the course.

So, based on previous experience and the belief that constructive feedback was important, I decided to experiment with the inclusion of a tool in my online and web-enhanced courses to encourage student feedback outside of the university-sanctioned student evaluations. Therefore, I incorporated the use of a Suggestion Box forum in the discussion area of the online course management system. I asked students to use the Suggestion Box to provide constructive feedback regarding the flow, the content, the textbook, the assignments, and any other aspects of the course they desired. Students were guaranteed anonymity in their postings as the appropriate settings were selected to ensure that no identifying information was available to me.

For almost two years, students posted nothing. No feedback of any type was found in any of the Suggestion Box forums for the classes I taught. Despite my reassuring students that any postings they made would be guaranteed anonymity and that I desired to know their opinions and wanted them to be engaged in discussions that would assist me in making decisions about their learning and how to improve learning opportunities for students moving forward, they did not respond. Until they did.

One fall semester, I got my wish. Students posted anonymous comments in the Suggestion Box. The class was Business Communication, and it was designated as web-enhanced, meaning tests and quizzes were given online, and all class materials were available in the online course management system. However, the class met in a face-to-face environment two times per week. At the beginning of the semester, I introduced students to the Suggestion Box forum in the discussions area. I explained its purpose and went over the parameters, defining constructive feedback and the types of information that would be of value to me in making changes or upgrades to the course. I never mentioned the Suggestion Box after that point and assumed that students knew its location and its purpose and would post feedback if they desired to do so.

Barely into the semester, a couple of my students stopped by to speak with me after class one day specifically to ask if I had been following the Suggestion Box postings. I explained that I had not looked at them as I tried to refrain from doing so until the semester ended. I wanted to give students time to navigate the entire course before reviewing the postings.

Of course, I didn't volunteer the information that I had never received any feedback in the Suggestion Box before, so I hadn't really needed to follow up on reading it. One of the students who had asked me whether I had been following the Suggestion Box then explained that not reading anything that was posted there was a good idea. The student went on to say that what had been posted was disgusting and that I should just ignore it. The other student who had also stopped to speak with me agreed, as did several others who remained in the classroom and overheard our conversation.

Well, when you tell me that I should not look at something, the message I hear is that I should read it right now. I thanked the students for their concern, and we left the classroom. I went straight to my campus office, logged into the course management system, and went to the Suggestion Box for my Business Communication course. As I began to read, my feelings flip-flopped from surprise and anger to hurt and dismay. I had never read such disrespectful comments from students. Oh, sure, I had the occasional "this class is too hard" or "you pay too much attention to grammar" type comments, but nothing that bordered on the personal attacks being launched by the anonymous postings in this Suggestion Box. I had just come face-to-face with incivility on a level with which I was totally unfamiliar. After reading these comments, I began to question my ability to teach. I had grave concerns about teaching the Business Communication class. I wrestled with the comments, had nightmares about them, woke up in the early morning hours (3 or 4 a.m.), and could not get the words to stop swirling through my brain. I was angry, upset, and hurt—all by turns, depending on where I was when those words entered my thoughts.

I wanted to confront the students who had posted the comments to the Suggestion Box, but I could not. Students were guaranteed anonymity for their postings. So, what was I to do? I had essentially allowed these students to control my Business Communication class and to impact me in such a way as to cause me to dread going to the class. My confidence was torn to shreds, and I was thinking about leaving the teaching profession.

After much weeping, wailing, and gnashing of teeth, I arrived at a decision. I could continue to allow these students to hold my Business

Communication class hostage, along with me, or I could confront this issue and use the postings for something better—something useful. I realized that I had a teachable moment, a way to discuss the use of performance appraisals in the workplace and how the use of tone in any message, particularly the written message, can impact the reader in ways far beyond what the writer might have perceived when constructing the message.

So, I did just that. I stood before my Business Communication class and shared the posts from the Suggestion Box and asked questions relevant to a performance appraisal. My students, particularly the ones who were concerned about the posts and how they might impact me, were very engaged in the discussion. They voiced their displeasure with how the posts were written, the tone of the messages, and what they conveyed about the writers. At the end of class, numerous students stopped by to speak with me about how well the class went and how appreciative they were of my sharing the posts and turning the lesson into something positive. I thanked them all for their concern and expressed my appreciation for their participation in the class discussion—and we never mentioned the Suggestion Box again that semester. In fact, I shut it down—not just in my Business Communication class but in all my courses for that semester. I have not used the anonymous Suggestion Box since. I haven't needed to.

Students provide plenty of feedback via e-mail about courses now, and most of it falls into the not-so-good category. Complaints abound regarding assignments, evaluation and grading techniques, and the amount of work required during the semester. I have been accused of using arbitrary and capricious grading techniques, giving too many assignments, having too much work in the course, not being responsive enough or not responding quickly enough, grading too harshly for the format, grammar, spelling, punctuation, and so on. Many of the messages I receive have hostile overtones. Many times, students simply skip the instructor stage and go straight to the dean of the college or the president of the university to complain about grades or some other act of malfeasance they deem to be occurring in a class. Incivility rules—and you don't always get a teachable moment.

By the way, I did find out who posted the messages in the Suggestion Box. I was able to obtain the names based on transmission control protocol/internet protocol (TCP/IP) addresses that students used to access the online course management system. The two students used the same computers and locations to access the Suggestion Box on each occasion, so determining their identities was not difficult. Both were University Honors College students, something that astounded me. I could not imagine ever speaking to a college instructor in that fashion, and most certainly not if I were accepted into the Honors College program.

Knowing their names, their majors, and bits of information about them, however, did not make their behaviors any more acceptable or palatable. In fact, I believe I felt worse—not for me, but for them. Without being able to personally discuss their behavior with them, did I do them harm? Did I miss the opportunity to help them gain an understanding of the difference between critical expression and incivility? I will never know, for they have long moved on postgraduation. I hope for their sakes that they have been successful in the workplace and in all other aspects of their lives. I also hope that they get an opportunity to read this book and recognize themselves in this Introduction and perhaps remember how their actions impacted me and other students. After all these years, I still remember, and I still feel the same sharp pang of disbelief and hurt because of their lack of civility and intent to harm.

We often never overcome acts designed to harm emotionally and psychologically because they impact our sense of worth and control—or lack thereof. For this reason, incivility in its pervasiveness damages society and creates a weakening of the human spirit, causing us to question our value and place in work and life. Therefore, whenever possible, we must ensure that civility is at the forefront of our actions regardless of the venue in which we are operating, whether virtual or real-time. To those who have suffered the incivilities of others, this book is dedicated to you.

CHAPTER 1

The Rise of Incivility

Many people believe that the rise in incivility is largely due to the proliferation of technology and the resulting development of social media. However, the decline in civility in Western culture began long before the advent of the computer, the Internet, or any other device or software application. Those advances simply made the practice of incivility easier, more prevalent, and more visible.

History of Incivility

To really understand incivility, we first need to focus on how to define it. We cannot address incivility or its meaning, though, without first looking at the history of etiquette and manners and the development of a civil society based on those norms and mores of culture that were deemed acceptable. Otherwise, how would we know when things began to go awry or when people became less civil?

Etiquette and Manners

The French have often been credited with the adoption of manners and the codification of social practices into a form called etiquette. However, if you review the historical background of etiquette and manners, you will find that the earliest record of an identified system of acceptable social practices is found in the writings of Ptahhotep, an Egyptian vizier in the third millennium BC. His writings focused on civil virtues toward others, perhaps the precursor to our "do unto others as you would have done unto you" philosophy.

Confucius, the Chinese philosopher, was another to address a code of morality for society, also adding rules for eating and speaking. Finally, the French king, Louis XIV, transformed these previous attempts to codify a system of morals and manners into his own method, one for demonstrating supremacy—his supremacy. King Louis used his set of rules for etiquette to remind any palace visitors of appropriate behaviors. He would print little tickets called etiquettes to stipulate where people could sit, the acceptable dress code for the occasion, and whatever other requirements he deemed necessary for taming the French nobility. Louis simply used etiquette as a means of solidifying his position as supreme monarch, but his rules spread throughout Europe because the dignitaries who visited the palace took these social norms with them when they returned to their homes. Rules of etiquette continued to spread in France during the 18th century especially among the upper class as a means of signifying status.

In the United States, George Washington (*Rules of Civility and Decent Behavior*) and Benjamin Franklin (Code of Morality) are both credited with writing codes of conduct to establish acceptable rules of etiquette in U.S. society. Washington's *Rules of Civility and Decent Behavior* contained 110 rules. Many of them still hold true in polite society today, for example, "If you cough, sneeze, sigh, or yawn, do it not loud but privately; and speak not in your yawning, but put your handkerchief or hand before your face and turn aside." Franklin's Code of Morality included 13 virtues and accompanying precepts such as "Moderation: Avoid extremes; forbear resenting injuries so much as you think they deserve."

In addition, the 19th century ushered in guidelines for children, providing rules for interactions with parents, teachers, and other adults, as well as each other. Today, many of the rules adopted in early etiquette would be deemed too harsh, overreaching, or absurd in their requirements. For example, one common etiquette guideline in the late 19th century included the admonition to avoid smiling for too long.

In 1922, Emily Post authored the book, *Etiquette in Society, in Business, in Politics, and at Home*, in which she covered social rules and manners. Her book began with the first chapter, "What Is Best Society?" in which she dispelled the notion that the best society meant a fellowship of the wealthy. Post directed her writing toward people she termed gentle-folk, people who were of good manners, understood social amenities, and had a natural inclination to be kind and considerate of others. She stated that etiquette included ethics as well as manners. Post's book remains in print today (with a shortened title, *Etiquette*), having been authored by her great-great-grandchildren, Lizzie Post and Daniel Post Senning.

Civility

While many believe that civility and etiquette are synonymous, they are thinking only in terms of the superficial construct of politeness indigenous to both. To fully define civility, we must delve into the true depths of the social contract that underlies the term. In other words, we must agree on what acceptable public behavior looks like, especially when expressing disagreement with others' opinions or beliefs.

The founders of the Institute for Civility in Government, Tomas Spath and Cassandra Dahnke, defined civility as the ability to embrace and express our beliefs or needs without degrading others' needs or beliefs in the process. Civility is more than manners, though, as to be civil means that we respect others' differences and have an appreciation for diversity. When we disagree with someone, we do not hate the individual or vilify the person for that opinion.

> *If civility is meant to be the zero point for appropriate behavior, then incivility undermines the rudiments of social order, and all is lost.*
> —Keith Bybee

Keith Bybee defined civility as "a code of public conduct." He went on to state that civility was not the only code to govern public conduct, as courtesy, politeness, chivalry, and gallantry are all mechanisms for managing behavior. Nonetheless, civility is the standard for all behavior, the baseline by which we live and interact. We can view civility in the most positive way as being the *threshold condition* that permits the types of interaction allowed by the other codes governing public conduct. However, as Bybee stated, "If civility is meant to be the zero point for appropriate behavior, then incivility undermines the rudiments of social order, and all is lost."

From Civility to Incivility

As mentioned earlier, incivility did not begin with the growth in technology. We have only to look at the history of the United States to find that belief at odds with social evolution in the nation. President John Adams and Alexander Hamilton exchanged numerous unkind remarks resulting in Hamilton writing a letter in October 1800 in which he labeled President Adams as a burden to his party. Hamilton continued his pattern of incivility with his duel with Aaron Burr, again the result of insults. Presidents John Quincy Adams and Andrew Jackson engaged in continual word assaults on each other, leading Jackson's supporters to blame Adams as the cause of the death of Jackson's wife due to his malicious treatment of her husband.

Historians agree that the mid-19th century was an era of incivility, with some actions extending beyond words and into the physical realm of fights and duels. Of course, with the looming Civil War as a backdrop for many of these actions, we can see how the growth of incivility was an expected outcome of the times. However, when people speak the truth or share an idea or opinion, they strengthen engagement; what causes a problem then is when that discussion devolves into chaos and physical response, when the language employed is uncompromising and hate-filled vitriol that is absent any attempt to consider another's idea or suggestion but instead is nothing more than shouting and name-calling. At that point, civil discourse has become impossible. Such was the case in 19th-century U.S. politics. At the same time, the 19th century has been designated the great age of etiquette education in the United States, with the publication of more than 236 manuals on manners and behavior occurring before 1900. Apparently, the demand for these publications was high as people attempted to navigate the proper ways to act at work, at play, when dating (or courting as it was known then), and visiting.

But how did we progress from political fights and verbal acts of aggression to everyday occurrences of incivility? One explanation given for the deterioration in manners and civility in American culture lies at the very heart of the origin of the country—the ceaseless need for change. The movement of settlers to the frontier, then the advent of the automobile that saw increased ease of mobility, and finally, just the simple restlessness of U.S. society led to the inevitable breakdown in civility. Transient people moving from place to place have no system of shared social relationships, thus fragile and tenuous civility. When people are entrenched in a location, the rules of etiquette and civility are more consistently observed.

In his book, *A Short History of Rudeness: Manners, Morals, and Misbehavior in Modern Behavior*, Caldwell discussed the rise in rudeness that marked the early years of the 20th century as a reckoning of a sort, one in which a sense of crisis about manners exploded via an abundance of articles in the nation's top magazines. Between 1900 and 1920, such articles published in *Ladies Home Journal, Harper's Weekly*, and *Century Magazine* assessed the state of American social behavior. As mentioned previously, Emily Post published her book, *Etiquette,* in 1922. However, her book contained references to the popular Victorian etiquette authority, the late Mary Elizabeth Wilson Sherwood (1826–1903). But that did not deter the popularity of Post's book as it quickly gained momentum in part due to Post addressing the widening chasm between good conduct and morality and how the two were becoming separated.

Impact of Incivility on Individuals and Organizations

Most people may not know of the Hawthorne experiments, especially if they are not business or psychology historians. The Hawthorne experiments took place at AT&T's Hawthorne plant in Cicero, Illinois. The Hawthorne plant was an equipment-manufacturing Western Electric division of AT&T, employing approximately 29,000 people. The Hawthorne experiments began in 1924 and concluded in 1933. Researchers from the Harvard Business School, led by George Elton Mayo, psychologist and professor of industrial research, studied workplace social behaviors and problems in management.

So, what led to this research project, and why did it take place in this quiet, unassuming suburb of Chicago? Al Capone is the answer. Capone established his headquarters in Cicero, commandeering the second floor of the Hawthorne Inn, effectively turning the town into one that civilized people avoided or sped through to escape the gunfire. Obviously, the backdrop of Al Capone's criminal enterprise was the perfect location for examining human relations in the work environment. Of course, that tongue-in-cheek explanation was not the reason the Hawthorne plant was chosen. What led to the Hawthorne experiment was the wide range of problems inherent in management and in the social behavior occurring inside the Hawthorne plant. The researchers were charged with examining relationships among variables such as physical conditions, job design, and management planning as they related to the factory's output.

What came out of the Hawthorne experiments really marked a change in how management's role was defined. Instead of being solely responsible for ensuring that workers understood how to perform their tasks and that they performed those tasks in an efficient manner, management's responsibility was to shape employees' mental attitudes and modify their social behavior by setting the company tone and building a civil community throughout the organization.

The Hawthorne studies, whose findings were noted for influencing Homans' social exchange theory (SET), were often questioned as to their validity. Many deemed them scientifically without merit, stating that the experiments raised questions more than provided answers. However, in identifying the impact of worker attitudes and interpersonal dynamics on the output of a factory, the researchers working as part of these experiments ushered in a *watershed* moment—spontaneous cooperation among individuals and between groups through interaction. Civil discourse through collaboration occurred organically.

However, despite the development of SET and its resulting implications, the rise in incivility among individuals and inside organizations continued after the Hawthorne studies had established a baseline for civil discourse and cooperation in the work environment. The element researchers likely failed to consider was human behavior and the tendency of some to act outside of established norms. Of course, in examining the decline in civility among individuals and organizations, you can ask yourself if people simply followed the guiding practice of ethical conduct called the Golden Rule—"do to others as you would have them do to you"—and considered their actions as if they were in the other person's place, wouldn't their behavior change? Could the answer be that simple?

We would like to think the answer is yes, but again, we are faced with human nature. We could exhaust ourselves in writing pages of text describing the incivilities inflicted on the public during the years leading up to the present day. That action would be outside the scope and purpose of this book. Nevertheless, we cannot fail to acknowledge that many of the actions of prior generations led to the decline in civility that currently permeates our society. For every fire, you must have a spark. When we fail to fully address the cause of the issue, hide it, or go so far as to fully welcome its presence into society, we cross a line that accepts acts of incivility without recourse. And then, incivility enters the organizations where we engage with co-workers, receive guidance from leaders, and basically spend most of our waking hours being pelted by a barrage of comments, criticisms, and rude acts. We have choices, of course: leave the job, develop stress-related health issues, or "do unto others" as they are doing unto us and engage in uncivil acts and behaviors in response or retaliation. Thus, the culture of one bad apple or the excuse that "everyone else does it so I'm just joining the rest of them" expands to encompass the entire organization.

References

"What Is Civility?" 2022. The Institute for Civility in Government. www .instituteforcivility.org/who-we-are/what-is-civility/.

American School of Protocol. 2020. *The History of Etiquette: Tracing Our Polite Past.* www.theamericanschoolofprotocol.com/post/the-history-of-etiquette-tracing-our-polite-past.

Bybee, K. 2016. *How Civility Works.* Stanford University Press. ISBN 9781503601543.

Caldwell, M. 1999. *A Short History of Rudeness: Manners, Morals, and Misbehavior in Modern America.* New York, NY: Picador USA/St. Martin's Press. ISBN 9780312263898.

Fadel, L. 2019. "In These Divided Times, Is Civility Under Siege?" *National Public Radio Special Series Civility Wars.* www.npr.org/2019/03/12/702011061/ in-these-divided-times-is-civility-under-siege.

Glassco, D.E. 2018. *Historical Incivility as a Foundation of America's Democracy.* https://deglassco.medium.com/historical-incivility-as-a-foundation-of-americas-democracy-pt-2-791064975c4b.

Miltimore, J. 2016. "13 Virtues in the Ben Franklin Code of Morality." *Intellectual Takeout: Feeding Minds, Pursuing Truth.* https://intellectualtakeout .org/2016/06/13-virtues-in-the-ben-franklin-code-of-morality/.

Minerd, J. 2000. "The Rise of Cyber Civility." *Futurist* 34, no. 1, p. 6.

Morris, J. 1996. "Democracy Beguiled." *The Wilson Quarterly (1976-)* 20, no. 4, pp. 24–35. https://doi.org/10.2307/40259363.

Orwin, C. September 1991. "Civility." *American Scholar* 60, pp. 553–564.

Post, E. 1922. *Etiquette in Society, in Business, in Politics, and at Home.* New York, NY and London: Funk & Wagnalls Company. www.gutenberg.org/ files/14314/14314-h/14314-h.htm.

Russell, P. 2020. *A Short History of Etiquette: Where Does Etiquette Actually Come From?* www.linkedin.com/pulse/short-history-etiquette-paul-russell/.

The Emily Post Institute. 2022. https://emilypost.com/.

Washington, G. 1888. *Rules of Civility and Decent Behavior*. A paper found among the early writings of George Washington. Washington, DC: W. H. Morrison. ISBN 9798710803707.

Wines, W.A. and M.P. Fronmueller. 1999. "American Workers Increase Efforts to Establish a Legal Right to Privacy as Civility Declines in U.S. Society: Some Observations on the Effort and Its Social Context." *Nebraska Law Review* 78, no. 3, pp. 606–643.

Zoller, Y.J. and J. Muldoon. 2019. "Illuminating the Principles of Social Exchange Theory With Hawthorne Studies." *Journal of Management History* 25, no. 1, pp. 47–66. https://doi.org/10.1108/JMH-05-2018-0026.

CHAPTER 2

Workplace Incivility

Julie Connelly had always believed the workplace to be one of the last strongholds of civility and that you could always count on people standing when a senior manager entered the room. People treated each other with respect. However, everything seemed to change, and she questioned if employees had become mad dogs in the office.

In a *Forbes* article, Julie Connelly proposed several reasons for the rise in workplace incivility:

- The flattening of the hierarchical structure with a focus more on teams has led to an absence of cues as to rank and seniority (e.g., to whom do we report).
- The informality of society at large has permeated the work environment and gotten twisted into self-centeredness.
- Society rewards people for confrontation and being competitive.
- The focus of companies has moved to profits over people (e.g., treat customers well but mistreat employees).

Any one of these potential issues can be destructive to an organization's human assets. Taken as a whole, they can bring a workplace to a standstill while managers and other leaders attempt to resolve conflicts between workers, handle real or threatening litigation, and/or expend resources and time needed to recruit and employ replacement workers.

Civility . . . is the sum of the many sacrifices we are called to make for the sake of living together. When we pretend that we travel alone, we can also pretend that these sacrifices are unnecessary.

—Stephen Carter

In an article in *Training*, Chris Lee speculated that for most, workplace incivility is not violence or harassment. He defined workplace incivility as the "thousand small slings and arrows" that eat away at the work environment and its employees. In contrast, though, Lee referred to Yale law professor Stephen Carter's book, *Civility: Manners, Morals, and the Etiquette of Democracy*, that warned against the belief that civility only refers to politeness or manners as the term means much more. In fact, Carter's definition of civility is perhaps more appropriate for our modern era and our daily workplace struggles: "Civility . . . is the sum of the many sacrifices we are called to make for the sake of living together. When we pretend that we travel alone, we can also pretend that these sacrifices are unnecessary."

Psychiatrist Edward Hallowell wrote an article for the *Harvard Business Review*, in which he discussed what he coined "the human moment," or the encounter between two people who share the same space and emotional and intellectual attention. In his opinion, simply sharing the same space was insufficient. Hallowell believed that people must engage in meaningful conversation without distractions. His concern hinged on the impact the absence of human moments would have on the workplace, especially long term. Co-workers could lose their sense of belonging and being part of the team; distrust, disrespect, and dissatisfaction could grow exponentially due to their contagious natures; and worst-case scenario, according to Hallowell, when the human moment vanishes, toxic worry fills the vacuum left in its place. Hallowell continued his explanation by stating that, unfortunately, people have allowed themselves to become too busy to engage with others in that human moment. We are too goal driven. We don't have time to be polite. Rudeness is acceptable, even glorified. We don't need civility.

For a population of workers who became isolated in cubicles and cars, in front of computer and television screens, whose interaction with people revolved around phone calls, e-mail, and other electronic shadows, we began to see the disintegration of human contact, the absence of a connection with others. Therefore, the belief that we were alone meant that we no longer needed to worry about our interactions with others. Civility steadily declined, replaced by *busyness* and the lean and mean mantra of the workplace.

James Morris took incivility a step further and called the 21st century the age of "whatever," a time when rudeness and nonchalance ruled. No one wanted to make a judgment or call conduct unacceptable. The workplace was filled with people who used demeaning language and offensive gestures and whose behaviors eroded moral values. Historians largely agreed, calling it the century of thoughtlessness and rudeness. Lynne Andersson and Christine Pearson stated in "Tit for Tat? The Spiraling Effect of Incivility in the Workplace" that the business world had long been considered the defender of civility where relationships between co-workers were friendly and polite. However, with the increased informality of society at large, Andersson and Pearson noted that businesses had started to experience the same changes in the work environment. After reviewing numerous publications dealing with the construct of incivility (*which Andersson and Pearson defined as rudeness and disregard for others; mistreatment that may lead to disconnection, breach of relationships, and erosion of empathy*) and its relationship to deviant and antisocial employee behaviors, Andersson and Pearson were ultimately able to arrive at a working definition of workplace incivility that focused on the violation of workplace norms designed to ensure mutual respect. Their belief was that by violating the basic principles for conduct in the workplace (e.g., the norms), any attempts at cooperation and motivation would be severely limited.

Christine Pearson, Lynne Andersson, and Christine Porath believed that workplace incivility disrupted work patterns and diminished the effectiveness of individuals who were the targets of the behavior as well as others in the workplace. So, to test their theory, they conducted interviews of 700 workers, managers, and professionals from a wide range of profit, nonprofit, and government sectors and sought questionnaire responses from an additional 775 employees from diverse organizations located across the United States, asking them to share their insights in understanding, recognizing, and managing workplace civility. In their published article, the researchers reported on five main issues: (1) defining workplace incivility, (2) profiling the instigator and the target of workplace incivility, (3) determining why incivility seems to be increasing in the workplace, and (4) uncovering the implications of incivility for employees and organizations, including (5) the effects of nonescalating, spiraling, and cascading exchanges.

The definition for workplace incivility remained largely unchanged from what Andersson and Pearson had previously stated in their article, "Tit for Tat? The Spiraling Effect of Incivility in the Workplace." However, they did call attention to the fact that while norms vary widely across organizations, the one common to every workplace is that of respect for fellow co-workers. In other words, organizations share a common moral understanding that allows organizational members to cooperate; and incivility violates this common workplace norm.

Also, Pearson, Andersson, and Porath discovered that incivility is often ambiguous and dependent on how the incident is viewed through the eyes of the target, the instigator, and any observers of the incident. The intent to harm is not as readily visible with incivility as with acts of aggression such as threats or sabotage or acts of violence such as physical assault or homicide. One person might behave uncivilly with intent to harm the target, and another person might behave uncivilly without intent (via ignorance or oversight). Thus, the ambiguity issue means the investigator must delve into the instigator and target to determine intent.

Most of the acts of incivility in the workplace came from a hierarchical position; the higher status of the instigator denotes superiority over the target. Regardless of their positions in the company, however, instigators were frequently described as temperamental, rude to their peers, disrespectful of others, and difficult to get along with. They were most often emotionally responsive to problems and viewed as sore losers. Many of these same individuals were reported by their co-workers as being especially cunning when relating to their superiors. These instigators tended to change their behavior when around their superiors, altering them significantly to suit what their superiors expected.

One of the major problems with workplace incivility as reported by Pearson, Andersson, and Porath is the cost to organizations. These costs accrue via increased absenteeism, reduced commitment, decreased productivity, or organizational departure, and they can be substantial. Many of these costs accrue outside of normal accounting practices, particularly the one related to organizational departure as targets often leave the job but not necessarily within the time closely associated with the incivility incident. When they depart, they quite often do not indicate that they are leaving because of the instigator or the incivility. Thus, when that information is not shared, the instigator is not held accountable for the behavior, and the organization does not have a record of the factual reason for the employee's departure. The organization loses.

Numerous potential explanations have been offered for the decline in civility in today's organizations. Charlie Gillis offered a three-part theory from the Johns Hopkins Civility Project, a think-tank that studied the influence of politeness on contemporary society: anonymity, stress, and narcissism. Dr. P. M. Forni, co-founder of the Johns Hopkins Civility Project, believed that the combined pressures of work and home were greater than ever, particularly among the growing number of single-parent households. Forni also believed that the self-esteem movement was largely to blame for the narcissism issue. In the 1970s and 80s, child-rearing and educational circles pushed for self-esteem development, thereby producing children (now adults) with supersized doses of self-absorption who are not attentive, considerate, courteous, or kind. In other words, they are narcissists of our own making.

Gillis stated that Forni raised some interesting points about the roots of incivility, particularly as to whether it is a learned behavior. He went on to further explain that Forni revealed in his publications that civility goes beyond class and manners but more into our emotional and spiritual well-being. He believed in connections between ethics, civility, and quality of life. Without civility, Forni said, people would be unable to build a socially supportive network necessary for their physical and psychological well-being.

If we take stress, one of the identified factors from the Johns Hopkins project, and examine it from the perspective of people who engage in uncivil behavior, what would we find? In an article in *The London Evening Standard*, Philip Broughton stated that over 60 percent of people blame bad behavior in the workplace on stress. According to these individuals, they simply do not have enough time to be nice. Donna Owens' interview of Jeannie Trudel, published in *HR Magazine*, revealed that accumulated stresses can affect organizational performance, including commitment, turnover and retention, and job execution. If left unchecked, incivility from accumulated stresses can extend into aggression or workplace violence.

While Christine Porath has conducted numerous studies on incivility in the workplace, including the high costs associated with increased incivility, her 2015 report homed in on the one element that resonated with employees: leaders need to show respect. Porath reported that of all the outcomes studied, none was more important to employees than being treated with respect. However, she continued by stating that in her studies over numerous years, she learned that most of the disrespect occurs because of a lack of self-awareness. People are unaware of how their actions affect others, failing to see how what they do or say can be perceived by others. Porath stated that many participants in her studies revealed that they simply did not have a role model for respect in their respective organizations.

In a published article, Lola Rasminsky discussed incivility's impact as the disregard for the value of others. She raised the question, "Who can feel safe in an environment where you know you could be undermined at any time?" This question goes straight to the heart of my experiences in higher education. One of the courses that I have taught for almost 30 years is business communication. This course helps college students hone their writing and communication skills for the workplace, moving the focus for those skills from the academic arena to the professional one. This course was once a requirement for all business majors at my university. Now, it is an option for a writing-intensive course that competes with others in the college of business and only among a few majors. Most of the departments have elected to remove business communication as a choice from their curriculum.

While the discussion was ongoing in my college as to the value of business communication to students majoring in business, why it should be part of the core, and what value it imparted to the college, my colleagues and I were subjected to comments denigrating our degrees, devaluing our program, and undermining everything that we stood for and worked for despite employers valuing communication skills and demanding better writing skills from college graduates. No one stepped in to change the discourse. So, we all know where we stood among our co-workers. We were unwanted, and if the opportunity presented itself, we would be removed from the college, possibly from the university.

So, do we have incivility in the university setting? Sure. According to Lola Rasminsky, when a leader makes incivility his personal policy, he sets the tone regardless of organizational structure, institution, or corporation.

And academic incivility is not a new concern. In fact, in 1999, the American Association of University Professors included incivility in its position statement, "On Collegiality as a Criterion for Faculty Evaluation." For many years, incivility was hidden under the term collegiality. Faculty were encouraged to be collegial in their dealings with one another, not intimidate colleagues or monopolize conversations. However, without applicable ground rules and leaders who demonstrate civil behavior, collegiality remains just another way of hiding behind a screen instead of bringing the offensive behavior into the open and calling it out.

Once an institution, organization, or corporation has become overrun with incivility, leaders will struggle to put the culture back on a more civil course. With cumulative skills such as writing or playing tennis, you become more proficient at them if you learn them correctly. If you do not learn them correctly, you will find yourself hard-pressed to correct any bad habits. The same is true of incivility. You will find preventing workplace incivility to be more efficient than attempting to correct it.

In 2020, the COVID-19 pandemic ushered in a new normal. Businesses were forced to close for several months, and employees worked from home. Parents had to homeschool their children and were often frustrated by the lack of support from school districts. Being isolated at home meant that they had limited contact with others; so, when businesses re-opened and employees returned to the workplace, they had lost their ability to engage in conversations or to cope with difficulties. Some had lost family members to COVID-19, and some were still engaged in homeschooling their children. Still others believed conspiracy theories and what online forums related about the virus, saying it was not as bad as experts said. Many employees were angry over mask mandates and opposed vaccine requirements. They felt powerless because of the constantly changing public-health policies. They lashed out and had numerous emotional outbursts.

The civility issues were present long before the COVID pandemic; however, according to Josephine Campbell, in her 2022 article titled "Work Incivility," human resource managers have seen an escalation of incivility between co-workers in the past two decades largely due to strongly held political beliefs. HR managers revealed that the best way to avoid some of the incivility in the workplace is to remind workers to

avoid specific topics that can lead to conflict, for example, religion, gender, and politics, to name a few. Nevertheless, when employees believe
the workplace has a political identity that differs from their own, conflict
arises. For example, if an employer shares political messages with staff,
employees may see this as representative of an organizational political
identity and perhaps one that is vastly different from theirs.

Social identity theory may be at the root of the incivility issue in some
organizations because people see themselves as members of social groups
that share common characteristics, usually similar beliefs such as racial, gender, or political ideas. Therefore, they see their co-workers as either like them
or not like them. If you have no control over the individuals with whom
you work, whether they are like you or not, then you are more likely to
engage in conflict because you will treat those you see as not being like you
in a negative fashion. So, even if employees are cautioned to avoid certain
topics in the workplace, social identity theory takes precedence over that
company policy. Incivility cannot always be governed by rules; sometimes
human behavior is more often dictated by membership in a social group.

Nevertheless, when asked, approximately 38 percent of Americans
stated that employers should take an active role in the eradication of
incivility from the workplace. Even though people desire to have
incivility addressed in the workplace, only three nationally recognized
incivility programs were on the radar as of 2018: The Veterans Health
Administration's *Civility, Respect, and Engagement in the Workforce*
(CREW); *Global Workplace Civility*, the Cisco Systems, Inc., program;
and Maimonides Medical Center's *Culture of Mutual Respect* intervention.

The VA's CREW initiative began in 2005 in response to employee
feedback that job satisfaction was being affected by low levels of civility.
Since its inception, over 1,200 VA workgroups have successfully implemented this program. Statistics show that in 2011, the VHA facilities
with the highest civility spent $2.2 million less on formal Equal Employ-
ment Opportunity claims and $26.2 million less in employee sick leave
costs compared to those VHA facilities with the lowest civility.

The Cisco Systems program no longer exists under its original title.
Instead, Cisco has invested in the development of a Conscious Culture in
which employees are encouraged to be empathetic, kind, and curious and
to continue learning.

Maimonides Medical Center in Brooklyn, New York, is required under its accreditation to meet two leadership standards related to disruptive and inappropriate behaviors. Leaders at Maimonides took the initiative to create a Code of Mutual Respect that included respectful behavior but also encouraged sensitivity and awareness of the causes of frustration that often led to inappropriate behaviors. Leaders of this initiative have tried various approaches to achieving their goals and have made modifications along the way to ensure their strategies could produce sustainable results. In the end, the culture of mutual respect should be the standard, and the Code of Mutual Respect would no longer be necessary.

Workplace Incivility and Customers

While I do not like to label students as customers, I can see how they could be called customers since they are purchasing services that allow them to acquire knowledge, skills, and abilities to become educated. So, in the interest of including them under this heading, I will temporarily pause my disapproval and use the term "customers" for college students.

Even though incidents of faculty incivility toward or against other faculty are not new, attacks against faculty by students have just recently begun to surface in publications and discourse. In fact, these acts of incivility have escalated over the past two decades, and they continue to rise.

College faculty continually complain about the absence of manners in today's college students. While the following generalizations about students are obviously not true for all, faculty as a whole agree that these behaviors are on the rise. Students have no problem getting in an instructor's face to voice complaints about grades—always unfair in their view. They show no respect for the boundaries of appropriate and acceptable comments. They challenge classroom behavioral rules and online course rules. They demand to be able to complete assignments in whatever fashion they deem best; whether the assignments conform to the instructions set forth or not is of no consequence. They complete the assignments; therefore, they should receive grades commensurate with their work regardless of what the professor expected from the assignments. College students believe they can (or should be able to) submit late assignments, take tests and quizzes at their leisure, and direct the class the way they desire—instructor be damned! And woe unto those instructors who dare to call them on their behavior or actions because RateMyProfessor is their favorite tool of retribution.

Are faculty seeing an increase in the number of bullying acts of college students against them? Or are college faculty more sensitive because of the number of acts of violence occurring on college campuses? Are these negative student behaviors the result of the customer service model that most colleges now employ? This model is one that students have seen employed by others (or themselves) to support the posting of anonymous complaints and hate-filled tirades against restaurants, grocery stores, law enforcement, shopping venues, hotels, airlines, churches, neighborhood associations, teachers, doctors, and/or lawyers—and many others—on social media.

Alternatively, are we dealing with some students who have adopted bullying as a way of life because it has worked for them—in elementary school, in middle school, in high school, and in their personal lives with family and friends? Perhaps what is occurring is the result of both the customer service model and the tendency to bully that is so pervasive in our society today. In essence, children learn what they live, so parents' constant threats to sue those who anger or upset them or who go to social media to post comments about businesses they feel have harmed them in some way might also form part of the basis of the bullying behaviors.

Parents have become part of the incivility issue in higher education as well. Even with the right to privacy for college students prohibiting faculty from sharing information with parents without a signed release from a student and/or the student's physical presence when speaking with a parent, parents still involve themselves in their students' college experience. One example provided by Jan Meires in a 2018 article related an incident with a student in a capstone nursing course. This student continually arrived late to class and was heard complaining to her classmates about the class being held on a Friday afternoon. She consistently blamed her low quiz scores on the instructor. When she failed the weekly quiz at the midterm, this student stood up in the class, threw her books to the floor, and began yelling at the teacher while rushing to the front of the classroom. As she stormed out of the room, she stated that she was going straight to the university president to complain about the horrible class, saying that she wanted the teacher fired.

In the meantime, the student called her mother to complain about the class and the teacher, leading her mother to make a frantic call to the university president. The student's mother complained about the teacher (who was failing her child) and demanded that the teacher be fired for incompetence. She wanted her child to have the best professor available because the one she had for the current nursing class is worthless.

After this incident, the teacher in this scenario opted to leave teaching, citing a general lack of student respect for her experience and teaching abilities. The teacher also stated in her exit interview that she received little support from university leadership to change the current oppressive climate. This example correlates with previous explanations regarding the importance of leadership demonstrating the practice of civility. When leaders allow incivility to be the acceptable condition, they encourage the increase of these behaviors. When people do not have to face any consequences for their actions, this lack of accountability emboldens them to continue their acts of incivility. In addition, others around them may be encouraged to do the same because they have observed the actions of one and realized the absence of consequences.

Additionally, we cannot overlook the interactions with customers that add another layer to the workplace challenges in organizations, institutions, corporations, and service industries, particularly during and after the COVID-19 pandemic in 2020. Engaging with the public following the long period of isolation when businesses closed their offices and employees worked from home left many business owners and managers clambering to handle increased incidences of incivility. Flight attendants and nurses were on the front lines of the most egregious acts of incivility; some were even physically assaulted.

While large companies must follow a different set of rules for engaging with customers—even the rude ones—smaller businesses can select customers by letting the uncivil ones know that they are too busy to serve them or refusing to take new clients. The selection process does not allow for bias and should not be driven by it but rather by well-defined expectations for customer behavior when engaging with employees of your organization.

Employees typically engage with customers in numerous ways, both in face-to-face settings and via apps, texts, and other virtual formats. When the COVID-19 pandemic forced everyone into their homes and closed businesses to in-person activities, an accompanying rise in incivility toward service employees including rude behaviors and comments, attacks, verbal aggression including threats, and passive aggression (e.g., eye rolls) was noted. A decrease in kindness and patience also followed on the heels of the COVID-19 pandemic. As such, customer behavior became an escalating problem for businesses affecting the global workforce. Service jobs in the United States represent 80 percent of total employment while accounting for similar percentages in Canada, the United Kingdom, Germany, and Israel. Therefore, with service jobs dominating, organizations must reframe their view of customers and replacing the traditional "the customer is always right" in today's workplaces.

Without addressing the *customer is king* model, companies are risking damage to both employees and the business. Employees who must deal with rude customers are the ones who also suffer from the emotional fallout, both from the encounter and from the repercussions of any actions they might take to speak up or push back against the customers' behaviors. Long-term exposure to this type of behavior results in lower production and engagement, faltering performance, and increasing employee attrition.

In addition, in service industries, the interaction between customers and employees is necessary for optimal performance. The two rely on each other for coproduction, so true quality customer service must have input and collaboration of both parties. Therefore, organizations must learn to manage customers to help improve their performance in the same ways they manage employees' performance.

One way organizations can both protect employees and promote appropriate customer interactions is through the development of policies and procedures for customers that address specific areas such as selection, training, evaluation, progressive discipline, and dismissal. When companies recognize that, like employees, not all customers are the right ones for their organization, they have taken the first step in the selection process to remove individuals who act uncivilly toward employees. Larger companies have been engaging in this process for some time, declining service requests, deciding which jobs to take, and so forth. Smaller companies, however, can take different approaches, such as letting uncivil customers know that your company is not presently taking new customers, stating that your company values frontline workers and will not tolerate their mistreatment, and creating marketing materials designed to attract customers who will adhere to your values. As long as your selection process is not driven by discrimination based on legally protected factors, you have the right to use well-defined expectations of civil behavior toward your employees for your customer selection process.

While you may think that training customers to be civil in their engagement with your employees is impossible, you need only think of the use of signage as a means of training the public. A perfect example is the Transportation Safety Administration (TSA) and its use of signs at airport security checkpoints warning passengers of fines and criminal penalties for threats, verbal abuse, and physical violence against its agents. Dairy Queen, in June 2022, began posting signs in its restaurants reminding customers to be patient and respect its staff, saying that for many of the employees, this job is the first they have held.

Evaluating customers may be difficult to envision. Nevertheless, that very process is being accomplished by companies such as Uber and Airbnb. These service platforms rate their customers, and these results are made public so that drivers and hosts can review them and then determine whether to offer service to these individuals if they have extremely low ratings or reviews that also include accusations of uncivil or abusive behavior. Knowing that they will be evaluated and that this information will be made public is often sufficient enough to remind customers that their behaviors and performance also matter. While your company may not use this type of system with which to evaluate customers, providing your employees with the ability to indicate when an interaction with a customer was problematic, whether abusive language or behavior was also involved, is critical to the employee's well-being as well as the company's continued health.

If, after attempting the selection, training, and evaluation processes, you find that your organization and its employees are still struggling with abusive and uncivil customers, you may need to take the final steps of progressive discipline, and that lead to dismissal. Your organization has the right to end a relationship with an abusive and uncivil customer. One example to consider is the zero-tolerance policy passed by the Federal Aviation Administration (FAA) in 2021 in the United States that was specifically designed to discourage unruly customer behavior on airlines. This policy involves potential fines or jail time for offenders. Other companies such as Amazon, McDonald's, Sephora, Facebook, Chili's, Wendy's, and JetBlue are firing bad customers. Some are banning customers due to violation of company policies or terms of service and user agreements; however, others choose the option due to repeated uncivil behaviors or at the discretion of the manager or owner.

Organizations that value employees must create a culture and environment that promotes safety and well-being. Doing so does not simply involve the internal operations of the organization itself but also the external constituents as well—customers, clients, students, and users. Having a plan in place, something to assist in modifying customers' behaviors toward employees, is no longer a suggestion but a necessity. We can no longer continue with the notion that the customer is always right because we know that to be an outdated model for customer service. Customers are now an integral part of the customer service process and must be coproducers of service. Doing so means practicing civility and compromise on both sides. When incivility is the rule, employers must have a mechanism for employees to use to handle those situations. Employees should not be the ones left to defend themselves without any support. Civility starts and ends with leadership.

References

"Civility, Respect, and Engagement in the Workplace (CREW)." 2011. *VA/VHA Employee Health Promotion Disease Prevention Guidebook.* Center for Engineering & Occupational Safety and Health, and Occupational Health Strategic Healthcare Group, Office of Public Health, Veterans Health Administration, U.S. Department of Veterans Affairs. www.publichealth .va.gov/docs/employeehealth/55-CREW.pdf.

Andersson, L.M. and C.M. Pearson. 1999. "Tit for Tat? The Spiraling Effect of Incivility in the Workplace." *The Academy of Management Review: Briarcliff Manor* 24, no. 3, pp. 452–471. Academy of Management.

Broughton, P.D. August 10, 2009. *Does Your Office Have Bad Manners? Incivility in the Workplace Is on the Rise and If Left Unchecked It Can Have Devastating*

Consequences for Staff Morale. Gale in Context: Opposing Viewpoints 28. London Evening Standard [London, England]. https://link.gale.com/apps/doc/A205506818/AVIC?u=tel_middleten&sid=ebsco&xid=156b49d4 (accessed October 22, 2022).

Campbell, J. 2022. "Workplace Incivility." *Salem Press Encyclopedia.*

Carter, S. April 10, 1998. *Civility: Manners, Morals, and the Etiquette of Democracy. Basic Books.* ISBN: 0465023843.

Connelly, J. November 28, 1994. "Have We Become Mad Dogs in the Office? I'm Afraid So. Reengineering Has Left Us Angry and Confused, and We're Starting to Vent Those Emotions on Each Other." *Fortune*, pp. 197–199.

Gillis, C. April 5, 2004. *Rude Awakening.* Gale in Context: Opposing Viewpoints 28. MacLean's. https://link.gale.com/apps/doc/A552130542/OVIC?u=tel _middleten$sid=bookmark-OVIC&xid=00d977da (accessed October 22, 2022).

Hallowell, E.M. 1999. "Human Moment at Work." *IEEE Engineering Management Review* 27, no. 2, pp. 29–34.

Kaplan, K., P. Mestel, and D.L. Feldman. April 2010. "Creating a Culture of Mutual Respect." *AORN Journal* 91, no. 4, pp. 495–510.

Lee, C. July 1999. "The Death of Civility." *Training*, pp. 24–30.

Meires, J. 2018. "Workplace Incivility: When Students Bully Faculty." *Urologic Nursing* 38, no. 5, pp. 251–254, 255. https://doi.org/10.7257/1053-816X .2018.38.5.251.

Morris, J. 1996. "Democracy Beguiled." *The Wilson Quarterly (1976-)* 20, no. 4, pp. 24–35. https://doi.org/10.2307/40259363.

Owens, D.M. February 2012. "Incivility Rising: Researchers Say Workers Might Not Have the Time to Be Civil." *HR Magazine*, p. 33.

Pearson, C.M., L.M. Andersson, and C.L. Porath. 2000. "Assessing and Attacking Workplace Incivility." *Organizational Dynamics* 29, no. 2, pp. 123–137.

Porath, C. May 2015. "The Leadership Behavior That's Most Important to Employees." *Harvard Business Review Digital Articles*, pp. 2–5.

Porath, C. November 2014. "Hal of Employees Don't Feel Respected by Their Bosses." *Harvard Business Review Digital Articles*, p. 205.

Rasminsky, L. March 25, 2017. "A Loss of Civility Goes Straight to the Bottom Line." *Globe & Mail* [Toronto, Canada] Gale in Context: Opposing Viewpoints B6. https://link.gale.com/apps/doc/A487003080/OVIC?u=tel_ middleten&sid=bookmark-OVIC&xid=8d9bbb1d (accessed October 22, 2022).

Scanlon, P.M. 2016. "Halting Academic Incivility (That's the Nice Word for It)." *The Chronicle of Higher Education* 52, no. 27, Gale in Context: Opposing Viewpoints A46+. https://link.gale.com/apps/doc/A448900533/ OVIC?u=tel_middleten&sid=bookmark-OVIC&xid=c1d57b6e (accessed October 22, 2022).

van Jaarsveld, D.D., D.D. Walker, and K.S. Kyung (Irene). November 22, 2022. "Encouraging Good Behavior From Your Customers." *Harvard Business Review*. The Big Idea Series/Incivility on the Front Lines of Business. https://hbr.org/2022/11/encouraging-good-behavior-from-your-customers.

CHAPTER 3

Development of Virtual Environments

The rise in incivility is inextricably linked to the expansion of virtual activity. Just as the problem of incivility did not emerge overnight, the virtual workplace did not arrive with the coronavirus pandemic in March 2020. In fact, e-mail is a form of electronic communication that has been around since the 1960s. It was first developed as a way for government researchers to communicate with each other, but it quickly became a popular way for people to communicate with each other in the general population. Today, e-mail is an essential tool for both personal and business communication.

We cannot discuss communication channels such as e-mail, however, without first addressing the development of the Internet. Without the Internet, none of these methods for communicating would have originated.

The Internet

While January 1, 1983, is considered the birthdate of the Internet, it started in the 1960s as a way for government researchers to share information.

- The Advanced Research Projects Agency Network (ARPANET) was one of the first wide-area computer networks in the world. It was developed by the United States Department of Defense in the late 1960s and was initially used by government researchers and academic institutions to communicate with each other.

- ARPANET is considered the precursor to the modern Internet as it employed many of the same technologies and principles that are still in use today.
- In 1990, Tim Berners-Lee, a scientist at CERN, the European Organization for Nuclear Research, set out to make the Internet more accessible and easier to use. He developed the Hypertext Markup Language (HTML), which became the platform used to create the World Wide Web. While many of us refer to using the Internet, we are really accessing and using the World Wide Web.

Electronic Mail

Ray Tomlinson is often credited with developing the first electronic mail (e-mail) system in 1971 or 1972, depending on which source you read; however, early e-mail was used at the Massachusetts Institute of Technology (MIT) in 1965. What MIT was using, though, was really a file directory system where an individual could put a message in another user's directory in a post where that person could see it when logging into the computer. This system was called MAILBOX and was much like leaving a note on someone's desk but involved computers on the same system only. These early e-mail systems were limited in scope and not widely used by the general population.

- Once computers gained the capability of talking to one another, the need to send e-mail to people outside of your own company and computer system arose. To accomplish this task, a process for indicating to whom the messages should go was needed—much like the postal system used addresses, the e-mail system needed an address process. Here is where Ray Tomlinson enters the picture. He is credited with inventing e-mail in 1971 or 1972. Tomlinson worked for Bolt Beranek and Newman as an ARPANET contractor.
- Tomlinson was the individual who established the e-mail address system, choosing the @ symbol randomly from the keyboard as a way of indicating sending messages from

one computer to another. The "@" symbol was used in programming to indicate a string of text and in e-mail was an easy choice for indicating the separation between a user's name and the name of the computer that individual was using, for example, name-of-the-user@name-of-the-computer.

- E-mail became mainstream as the technology behind it improved and as more and more people began using it. In the early days of e-mail, it was primarily used by government researchers and other academic communities, but as technology developed and became more user friendly, it began to be used by a wider audience.

- The development of the modern Internet in the 1980s also played a role in the widespread adoption of e-mail as it made e-mail easier for people to access and use from anywhere.

- Today, billions of people around the world use e-mail for communication. In fact, many users receive 1,000 e-mails per day, with computer systems often processing millions of messages per day, delivering these messages within minutes or seconds, all while experiencing only a tiny fraction of failed deliveries.

Instant Messaging

Instant messaging (IM) is defined as a form of text-based communication between two persons engaged in a single conversation via computers or mobile devices within an Internet-based chat room. IM differs from chat due to the privacy of the communication. Chat typically involves a wider audience and is open for participation to many.

- IM was first launched in 1969 when a UCLA student, Charley Kline, attempted to send a message to a computer at the Stanford Research Institute over the first link on the ARPANET. However, IM did not enjoy broad-based use until the launch of AOL Instant Messenger (AIM) in 1997. With its use of proprietary OSCAR instant messaging, AIM allowed users to communicate in real time. Users had a Buddy

List and could hear doors opening and closing when contacts on that list signed in or out. AIM remained popular until the development and launch of other IM programs led to its demise.

- Statistics revealed that at the height of popularity, 41 million messages were sent every minute, with over 2.9 billion people using Messenger (a Facebook product) and WhatsApp, the two most popular IM programs. In the United States, 2.52 billion people used messaging apps on their mobile phones, with Messenger being the most popular app, with 107.87 million users.

- In addition, 20 billion messages per month were exchanged between businesses and users via Messenger. This figure is astounding as it showed that communication is largely virtual in the business environment relying heavily on the written word rather than on face-to-face or spoken means that allow for the inclusion of nonverbal communication to complement the message. However, the addition of emojis to the IM platform can help to combat the absence of personal presence.

- Emojis are defined as a small digital image or icon used to express an idea or emotion in electronic communication. Emojis are often used in text messages, on social media, and in other forms of online communication—such as IM—to add tone and emotion to a message. They are a popular way to add personality and flair to written communication and are often used to replace words or convey emotions that might be difficult to express using text alone. Emojis are standardized across platforms so that the same emoji will appear the same way on all devices. An important point to note about emojis, though, is that they can be misused or overused; so, just because they are available, we must use them carefully and appropriately in communication. Consider your reader and the reader's background before deciding to use an emoji. Not every culture defines emojis' meanings in the same way. What might appear to be funny, sincere, or nonthreatening to one person might have a very different meaning to another.

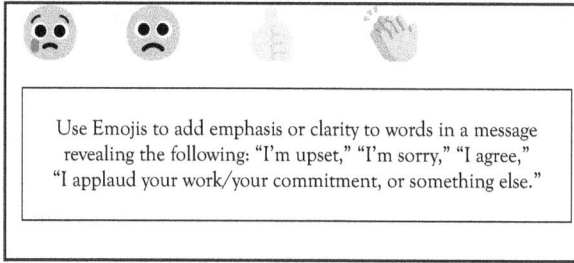

Use Emojis to add emphasis or clarity to words in a message revealing the following: "I'm upset," "I'm sorry," "I agree," "I applaud your work/your commitment, or something else."

Chat

In 1988, the first Internet Relay Chat (IRC) was created by Jarkko Oikarinen at the University of Oulu in Finland. Oikarinen designed the IRC to support bulletin board functions that allowed people to discuss news, software, and other issues online. This original chat room platform had only one server and one network.

- James Gosling led a team of computer engineers at Sun in 1991 to develop a programming language originally called Oak. By 1995, however, the program had been renamed to Java. Java made possible the creation of dynamic graphics and applications on the Internet leading to the development of numerous websites creating Java chat rooms. Java chat could be embedded into a web page so that people could participate in chat rooms from their Internet browsers.
- In 2001, AOL offered users its 2.0 version of AIM that allowed non-AOL subscribers to use the messenger and included the use of private chat rooms. Yahoo! Messenger was launched in 1998.
- Chat rooms have not disappeared; they have merely morphed into tools used by businesses. You still have apps designed for friends to chat with one another or for those who want to keep in touch with international friends and acquaintances. However, you also have apps that allow business teams to work together and for businesses to talk to their customers. Many organizations are simply integrating chat into their website so that customers or clients can send an inquiry

without the need to download an app or searching for a specific form to complete. What is termed "live" chat is very useful to businesses. The benefits are numerous when customers can instantly connect with a business representative to have a question answered or to make a request. These live chat specialists create personal connections with customers in ways that texts or e-mails cannot. When asked their preferences for communication with companies, 42 percent of all customers stated their preference for live chat over all other communication channels.

- Chat rooms have evolved to include capabilities such as screen sharing, real-time translation, and screen captioning. Many of them allow for customization to match companies' website designs and branding. In addition, the latest feature to become part of a select few chat room programs is that of artificial intelligence. One such program, Smith.ai, advertised itself as a virtual receptionist and lead intake software.

- Chat as a communication tool continues to grow and evolve. Businesses and individuals benefit from its development and likely will do so for many decades to come. While the iterations of chat will likely change its appearance and implementation, its usefulness and inclusivity in our day-to-day life will only increase due to its ease of use and speed in communicating with others. We live in a world where the need for instantaneous responses and timely updates dominates our day-to-day activities. Chat fills that need.

Social Media

Social media refers to websites and applications that enable users to create and share content or to participate in social networking. This process typically involves creating a profile, adding a network of friends or followers, and posting content that others can comment on, like, or share. Some examples of social media platforms include Facebook, Instagram, LinkedIn, Snapchat, and Twitter. These platforms can be used for a variety of purposes such as keeping in touch with friends and family, networking professionally, and following news and current events.

Few people are aware of the roots of social media, believing that they originated in 1997. However, a brief review of its history reveals that social media, in a sense, began on May 24, 1844, with a series of dots and dashes tapped out on a telegraph machine. Samuel Morse sent the first electronic message—"What hath God wrought?"—from Baltimore to Washington, DC, using a series of codes representing letters of the alphabet.

Following Morse's invention, telegraph operators used his code to chat with one another by tapping messages on their telegraph keys. All operators along the line could hear everything that was transmitted and could join the unofficial conversation, thus establishing a shared chat room. The operators even developed their own shorthand or brief forms for expressions: GM meant good morning; SFD meant stop for dinner. They played chess and checkers using Morse code, became friends without ever meeting, and even developed romances in this virtual world. According to the "History of Social Networking," everything began with the Bulletin Board System (BBS). These online meeting spaces allowed users to communicate with a centralized system that would allow them to download files or games and post messages to other users. BBSs were accessed via phone lines using a modem, and since many required long-distance calls (with long-distance calling rates applicable), many Bulletin Boards became locals-only networks.

Despite their shortcomings regarding flexibility and text-only exchanges—not to mention the snail's pace speed at which they operated—they gained in popularity through the decade of the 1980s and well into the 1990s.

- **CompuServe**. In fact, one such program, CompuServe, began in the 1970s as a business-oriented mainframe computer communication solution. However, in the late 1980s, CompuServe expanded into the public domain and offered something to users that had never been experienced—true interaction. You could share files, access news and events, but you could also send a message to a friend via e-mail or join any of CompuServe's thousands of discussion forums to engage with other members.

- **America Online (AOL)**. Notwithstanding these profound technological developments, the true precursor to today's social networking sites was likely America Online (AOL). AOL had member created communities with searchable member profiles. What followed was an explosion of social networking sites.
- **Yahoo and Amazon**. By the mid-1990s, Yahoo was on board, and Amazon had just begun selling books.
- **Classmates.com**. By 1995, the site was created that may have been the first to meet the modern definition of social networking. Classmates.com differed from many current social networking sites because it focused on connecting with former classmates. While early users of this program could not create user profiles, they could search for people with whom they had attended school. Classmates.com was an instantaneous success. In 2016, the site had approximately 57 million registered accounts.
- **Friendster**. Social networking continued to experience unprecedented growth, and in 2002, with the launch of Friendster, it seemed to have found its niche. Within a year of its launch, Friendster had more than three million registered users.
- **LinkedIn**. In a bid to move toward a more professional platform, LinkedIn was introduced in 2003 as a networking resource for businesspeople wanting to connect with other professionals. As of May 2023, LinkedIn has approximately 930 million members around the world.
- **MySpace**. Also introduced in 2003 was MySpace, the one-time favorite social networking site. MySpace competed with Friendster and was seen as hipper right from the start. In fact, it conducted a campaign to show alienated Friendster users what they were missing by not using MySpace. Friendster eventually abandoned social networking and operates today as only an online gaming site.

- **Facebook**. MySpace met Facebook in 2006 when the new competitor was finally opened to the general public. Facebook was launched by Harvard University students in 2004 as a Harvard-only exercise, remaining as a campus-oriented site for two years. However, by the time Facebook was available to the general public, its reputation had already preceded it. Numerous wealthy investors provided tens of millions of dollars to ensure the social networking site flourished. Facebook's success is attributed to one thing: Facebook promotes both honesty and openness. Users seem to enjoy being themselves, being open about their thoughts, and sharing that information for all to see. As of May 2023, Facebook has approximately two billion users around the world. MySpace is now a social networking site for bands and musicians only.

- **Twitter**. While Facebook was under development and in use on the Harvard campus, Twitter was emerging from the podcasting venture Odeo. Evan Williams, Biz Stone, and Noah Glass had debuted a version of Twitter in July 2006 and believed that the product had a promising future that they needed to explore. So, they bought Odeo in October 2006 and began Obvious Corp. By purchasing Odeo, they were able to further develop Twitter. They presented Twitter at the South by Southwest Music and Technology conference in Austin, Texas, in March 2007. An infusion of venture capital followed; and the following month, Williams, Stone, and Glass founded Twitter, Inc.

  ○ Initially, Twitter was perceived as a free IM program with limitations for posts (called tweets) of 140 characters. It also possessed an element of social networking but lacked a clear focus and was seen as more of a curiosity. Nonetheless, Twitter saw an increase in visits of 1,300 percent in 2009 and in April 2010 unveiled its new advertisement campaign designed to be a primary revenue source.

  ○ Twitter's social networking roots were clearly unveiled in 2009 when actor Ashton Kutcher competed with news network, CNN, to see which could obtain more than one million followers. Kutcher emerged the victor in that competition. Following on the heels of Kutcher's victory, businesses began using Twitter to send promotional tweets, and political campaigns used tweets to communicate with the population of voters. In fact, former U.S. President Barack Obama dominated all social media in his 2008 campaign. His use of social media platforms ensured that future political campaigns would include a presence there as part of their media strategies.

º Where Twitter truly began to shine, however, was as an outlet for journalists. It became an up-to-the-second tool for sharing information that transcended all political borders. The first tweet that shared a current news item occurred on January 15, 2009, when Janis Krums broke the story of the U.S. Airways Flight 1549 water landing on the Hudson River in New York City. The tweet included a snapshot of passengers disembarking onto the wings of the plane in the middle of the river.

º After the U.S. Airways incident, Twitter doubled down on becoming the emerging outlet for dissemination of information. The events surrounding the Iranian presidential election in June 2009 and the 2010 earthquake in Haiti were both covered on Twitter. When foreign journalists were forbidden from covering opposition rallies in Iran, Twitter (and other social networking sites) filled the gap. Twitter once again demonstrated its versatility during the 2010 earthquake in Haiti by both reporting on the tragedy and helping the Red Cross launch a fundraising campaign that eventually surpassed all expectations.

º Twitter became a public company in 2013 but initially failed to become profitable. So, in 2017, the character limit of tweets was doubled from 140 to 280, and several other changes were made to the platform to make it more relevant and to encourage users to interact more. Twitter finally became profitable in the last quarter of 2017. In September 2022, Twitter was purchased by South African-born American entrepreneur Elon Musk.

- **Instagram, Snapchat, Reddit, Pinterest, and TikTok.**
Many other social media/networking platforms have joined Facebook and Twitter—Instagram, Snapchat, Reddit, Pinterest, and TikTok, to name a few. Some of them are about photo sharing and video sharing, others involve pinboards and stories. They have all joined the mobile movement and created applications so that their experiences can be taken to phones and tablets, and users' communities can go with them wherever wireless networks and cellular service are found.

While the initial purpose of social media and networking was to connect users with friends, colleagues, family, and like-minded individuals, they have now morphed into tools useful to social media users interested in travel, entertainment, fashion, and other visually appealing topics. Businesses have found uses for social media to help them grow their customer bases and gain access to data that previously were unavailable. Companies can grow their brand awareness, generate leads, develop and maintain relationships with customers, and learn from their competitors, all with a few clicks of the keys on a laptop, mobile phone, or tablet.

Virtual Meetings and Presentations

When we mention virtual meetings or virtual presentations, most people's thoughts immediately go to Zoom, the most used platform in 2022 for participating in online meetings or for delivering presentations. However, if you examine the roots of virtual meetings and presentations, you find audioconference and videoconference references dating back to the 1800s.

You know that humans are never satisfied with the status quo. We are always looking for something better than what presently exists. So, when the telephone was invented in the late 1800s, it wasn't long before people began to express dissatisfaction with just hearing the other person. They wanted to see the other person. Obviously, that process did not happen overnight and took some decades of research and development before video transmission was possible.

- With the invention of the telephone, audio transmission became a relatively simple process. When attempting to add the video component, though, the camera became the villain. Stable and operational television cameras did not become available until the 1920s, so attempting to create any type of videoconferencing was impossible until that time. In its first attempt, AT&T Bell Telephone Laboratories broadcasted a live moving image of then Commerce Secretary Herbert Hoover from the White House to New York on April 7, 1927. Viewers in a New York auditorium located some 200 miles from the White House could see Secretary Hoover, but he could not see them.

- AT&T tried again in 1931 when it demonstrated a two-way video communication session between two of its offices, both located in Manhattan, New York. In this attempt, both parties could see each other. Despite this successful attempt, efforts to further develop videoconferencing were delayed due to the effects of the Great Depression, and nothing further was attempted until 1936.

- During the 1936 summer Olympics in Germany, a German inventor named Georg Schubert demonstrated the use of a modern video telephony he called the visual telephone system. His visual telephone system required the use of coaxial cable transmission lines. So, the first connection was between Berlin and Leipzig, about 100 miles apart. As his visual telephone system worked, coaxial cable transmission lines were eventually expanded to more than 620 miles. Video call booths were set up in post offices in cities located on 620 miles of coaxial cable transmission lines so people could visit the call booths and connect to call booths in other cities. With the start of World War II, though, the visual telephone system was discontinued in Germany.

- Moving forward in the United States, Bell Telephone Laboratories developed a prototype of a two-way communication system in

1959. The transmission was slow and able to transmit only one frame every two seconds. However, the image was clear and stable. AT&T called this project the Picturephone Mod I. A working videophone was presented at the 1964 World's Fair in New York on April 20.

- AT&T continued to refine the Picturephone and, in 1969, unveiled the Picturephone Mod II. This videophone was designed to be an office video communication system that could broadcast 30 frames per second, much faster than its predecessor. Nevertheless, the attempted national rollout of the Picturephone network failed.

- Compression Labs, a competitor of AT&T, created CLI T1 in 1982. It was heralded as the first commercial group videoconferencing system. The drawbacks to the CLI T1 were its size (the hardware needed an entire room), its initial investment cost ($250,000), and its user cost ($1,000 per hour). While the CLI T1 may have been a formidable product, the demand for videoconferencing systems had not reached the height required to outweigh the negatives associated with acquisition of it.

- In 1984, a group of MIT students and their professor formed the PictureTel Corporation. They invented the first commercial video codec that would ensure more efficient data transfers. AT&T chose PictureTel in 1989 for an international videoconference to provide two-way, real-time audio and full-motion video connections between PictureTel headquarters and the AT&T office in Paris, France. PictureTel became an IBM multimedia business partner in 1991.

- Cambridge University Computer Science Department students invented the first web camera (webcam) in 1991, and a Cornell University student wrote a program, CU-SeeMe, in the early 1990s as well. The CU-SeeMe program became the first desktop videoconferencing platform. In 1994, Connectix began selling QuickCam, the first commercial webcam. Logitech purchased the QuickCam. Polycom released its SoundStation in 1992. SoundStation was a triangular speakerphone with high-quality audio that enabled both parties (caller and receiver) to simultaneously speak and be heard.

With the rise of the smartphone came the rise in videoconferencing. When smartphone technology evolved to include front-facing cameras, especially with the introduction of the iPhone 4 and FaceTime, video-conferencing really took off. Initially, smartphones had to be connected to Wi-Fi for videoconferencing; however, Apple quickly realized the need for the addition of cellular service options and added support for those as well.

Skype was first introduced in 2003 and became the "go-to" tool for videoconferences and meetings of all types. eBay bought Skype in 2005 and sold it to Microsoft in 2011. However, the oldest videoconferencing platform or tool is WebEx. It was developed in 1995 and acquired by Cisco Systems in 2007. WebEx offered a suite of products for business users. However, in September 2020, Cisco launched WebEx Classrooms for virtual homerooms. BlueJeans, another videoconferencing tool, began in 2009. It was acquired in May 2020 by Verizon Communications. Microsoft introduced Microsoft Teams in 2017 as a replacement for Skype for Business and Microsoft Classroom. The Teams platform has individual and group chat, file sharing, team channels, and real-time text transcriptions of voice chats.

The 2020 COVID pandemic led to the need for videoconference platforms that allowed people to work from home and for children to attend school online. Videoconferencing tools gained in popularity but none more so than Zoom Cloud Meetings or Zoom as it is most often called. Zoom's developer pushed out new features almost monthly to keep up with demand for the product. In fact, Zoom has become a household name, becoming so well known that it is now used as a verb as well as a proper noun.

The demand has continued despite the return to work and school. Many employees and employers have opted for the work-from-home hybrid model, so they continue to need and use a videoconference platform. Many schools saw the benefits of developing and maintaining online courses and programs because they also fill the gap for students who are injured or ill and unable to attend classes on campus. Additionally, what once was thought of as only an in-person event or opportunity can now be seen as having a viable virtual component. For instance, graduations, weddings, and funerals can now be live streamed for those who cannot or who do not wish to travel.

Some of the other work-oriented videoconferencing and meeting tools in use include the following:

- *RingCentral Video.* This videoconferencing program integrates with other productivity tools such as Slack, Google Workspace, and Microsoft 365. RingCentral was selected as best overall videoconferencing tool in 2023 by FounderJar.
- *Dialpad Meetings.* Considered a top videoconferencing platform, this program has built-in artificial intelligence tools (e.g., real-time transcriptions) that lead to better meeting recordings.
- *Lifesize.* When looking at cloud-based collaboration platforms, Lifesize is considered best for scalability because it allows users to host an unlimited number of video calls and does not impose any meeting length on those calls.
- *Whereby.* For hybrid meetings, Whereby is deemed a suitable videoconferencing software. This program allows users to integrate real-time video calls into product pages or websites.
- *Zoho Meeting.* This browser-based platform allows users to host videoconferences and webinars. Other videoconferencing platforms are much more extensive; however, Zoho Meeting helps small businesses perform these tasks at a much more affordable cost.
- *ClickMeeting.* The best platform for events and webinars is ClickMeeting. This online meeting, webinar, and virtual event platform can be used to host online courses and training sessions, product demonstrations and meetings, online business meetings, and even large-scale online events.
- *GoToMeeting.* This easy-to-use online meeting platform was formerly known as Join.me. Called the best mobile-friendly videoconferencing app, GoToMeeting allows remote workers to use engaging and collaborative web conferencing tools (e.g., real-time screen sharing and integrated audio).

- *Microsoft Teams.* This videoconferencing platform is best for Microsoft 365 app integration. This platform can host up to 10,000 participants, and users can share their screens, change their backgrounds, and receive calls directly in the app. Microsoft Teams is widely used in educational institutions that have adopted Microsoft 365.
- *Cisco WebEx.* Named the best videoconferencing app with the highest video quality resolution, Cisco WebEx is outstanding for online training, webinars, remote support, and businesses having legitimate security concerns. Users can host virtual events with up to 1,000 attendees.

Virtual meetings and conferences are not likely to disappear. In fact, the technologies will evolve to include other features to make them more functional and easier to use. Pros and cons will always exist for videoconferencing, but as developers move forward with improvements to their platforms and companies reduce the costs associated with their use, the very nature of communicating with people who are visible is better than just words on a screen via e-mails, texts, or instant messages. You can include nonverbal communication in visual encounters to help reduce misunderstandings, and that is a good first step toward maintaining a civil environment.

Online Learning Management (Course Management) Systems

An online learning management system (sometimes referred to as a course management system) or a virtual learning environment (VLE) is a platform that allows teachers to create and deliver course content, manage student progress, and assess student performance. These systems are typically accessed through the Internet (usually through school systems or university/college websites) and are designed to support distance learning and blended learning environments. They often include a range of features, such as the ability to upload and share documents, create and grade assignments, conduct online discussions, and hold virtual class meetings. The main goal of an online learning management system is to provide a centralized, convenient, and user-friendly platform for managing and delivering educational content.

- Modern learning management systems got their start with the teaching machine that was developed by Sidney L. Pressey in the 1920s. The teaching machine resembled a typewriter but offered various kinds of practical exercises and multiple-choice questions that required learners to fill in answers instead of typing them out. Answers were recorded at the back of the machine. Learners could only advance if their responses to questions were correct.
- In 1929, Milton Ezra LeZerte created the problem cylinder. It was a device that provided instruction without a teacher's intervention. The problem cylinder tested learners' knowledge via multiple-choice questions, but it also checked their responses so that the instructor did not have to do so.
- The University of Houston televised the first for-credit college course in 1953. People were able to take the course from the comfort of their own home as video lectures and lessons were televised each weeknight so that anyone, including full-time workers, could benefit from this opportunity.
- **SAKI**. In 1956, Gordon Pask and McKinnon Wood introduced the Self-Adaptive Keyboard Instructor (SAKI). SAKI offered personalized practice questions based on the learner's performance. It would learn and increase the complexity of questions as the learner's performance improved.
- **PLATO**. The invention of PLATO (Programmed Logic for Automatic Teaching Operation) in 1960 provided the learning community its first opportunity to experience social or collaborative learning. PLATO had a host of networks so learners could interact with other learners using instant chat and messaging, e-mail, and chat rooms. PLATO debuted at the University of Illinois at Urbana-Champaign and continued to offer coursework for four decades before being purchased as a commercial product. This system has been

called the precursor for learning management systems because many of the concepts that it pioneered are those that are in use for learning management systems today.

- **FirstClass**. Following PLATO, came what was called the first real learning management system, FirstClass. FirstClass was released in 1990 by SoftArc and was designed to run on personal Macintosh computers (Apple). FirstClass supported private e-mail and public forums that allowed students to ask questions and clarify information presented in the learning modules.

- **Moodle**. The first open-source learning management system, Modular Object-Oriented Dynamic Learning Environment or Moodle, was released in 2000. It continues to be one of the most popular open-source systems available online.

- **WebCT**. WebCT (Web-Based Course Tools) joined the learning management systems fray in early 1996. It was originally developed by Murray Goldberg, a faculty member in computer science at the University of British Columbia, in response to his research showing that student satisfaction and academic performance could be improved by using a web-based educational resource or WebCT.

  ○ Goldberg presented the first version of WebCT at the fifth International World Wide Web Conference in Paris in 1996. WebCT grew in popularity to the point where it was in use by over 10 million students in 80 countries. However, as with many competition situations, WebCT was acquired by its rival Blackboard, Inc. in 1996, and the name was phased out in favor of the Blackboard brand. Many WebCT users moved away from Blackboard to open-source learning management systems.

- **Brightspace (Desire2Learn)**. Other learning management systems have entered the market since WebCT and Blackboard. One such system is Desire2Learn (now known as Brightspace). Most of the current learning management systems are cloud-based and offer similar tools. The platforms are easy to use and designed to provide support and flexibility for learners. These learning management systems provide chat rooms, discussion forums, and many other tools to enhance collaboration and communication. Brightspace, for example, also provides a video note tool with which teachers or students can record short video notes to introduce themselves, or to provide feedback on assignments, or to ask questions about assignments. These video notes are an excellent alternative to the text-based e-mail or discussion forums because learners can see and hear the message rather than simply read it, an especially helpful way to avoid confusion or the appearance of incivility because of misunderstanding a written message.

Now that we have looked at the types of virtual environments and brief histories for the development of each, we can shift our focus to the growth of the remote workplace and its rise in popularity. Taking what we learned about the online tools and platforms in this chapter and applying it to individuals working remotely helps us navigate the path to better understanding the rise in incivility and its acceptance in the online environment. In the next chapter, we will look at the development of remote working and the driving influences that led to its acceptance and growth. From that viewpoint, we will begin to see the underpinnings of incivility take root.

References

"The Evolution of Social Media: How Did It Begin, and Where Could It Go Next?" 2022. Maryville University. https://online.maryville.edu/blog/evolution-social-media/.

Athmika, T. November 25, 2021. *A Brief History of the Learning Management System (LMS)*. CommLab India. https://blog.commlabindia.com/elearning-design/learning-management-system-evolution.

Belyh, A. April 5, 2023. *11 Best Video Conferencing Software Platforms of 2023*. FounderJar. https://www.founderjar.com/best-video-conferencing-software/.

Damjan. March 29, 2022. *Text, Don't Call: Messaging Apps Statistics for 2022*. https://kommandotech.com/statistics/messaging-apps-statistics/.

Fitzgerald, Q. May 2, 2023. *Facebook Statistics 2023: How Many People Use Facebook?* https://quantummarketer.com/facebook-statistics/.

LinkedIn Pressroom. May 2023. *About Us: Statistics*. https://news.linkedin.com/about-us#Statistics.

Maize. April 23, 2020. *A History of Instant Messaging and Chat*. www.maize.io/news/lizshemaria-historyof-instant-messaging/.

Mears, L. and S. Dutfield. March 31, 2022. *World Wide Web: Definition, History, and Facts*. www.livescience.com/world-wide-web.

Patrizio, A. August 17, 2021. *The History and Evolution of Video Conferencing*. WhatIs.com. www.techtarget.com/whatis/feature/The-history-and-evolution-of-video-conferencing.

Rosenwald, M.S. May 24, 2017. "Before Twitter and Facebook, There Was Morse Code: Remembering Social Media's True Inventor." *The Washington Post*. www.washingtonpost.com/news/retropolis/wp/2017/05/24/before-there-was-twitter-there-was-morse-code-remembering-social-medias-true-inventor/.

Science+Media Museum. December 3, 2020. *A Short History of the Internet*. www.scienceandmediamuseum.org.uk/objects-and-stories/short-history-internet.

Shah, S. May 14, 2016. *The History of Social Networking*. DigitalTrends. www.digitaltrends.com/computing/the-history-of-social-networking/.

Sharma, A. 2016. *The History of Distance Learning and the LMS*. eLearning Hub. https://elearnhub.org/the-history-of-distance-learning-and-the-lms/.

Taylor, A. 2022. *The Key Benefits of Live Chat for Businesses*. Ruby. www.ruby.com/blog/key-benefits-live-chat-businesses/.

Twitter. 2022. *Encyclopedia Britannica*. www.britannica.com/topic/Twitter.

CHAPTER 4

The Rise of the Virtual Workplace

Just as incivility has its roots in an earlier time, so too does the virtual work environment. Remote work began approximately two centuries ago at the height of the Industrial Revolution. Obviously, our definition of virtual work differs from that time to some degree, but many people currently sell their products from the comfort of their homes just as craftsmen did hundreds of years ago. However, they have technology to aid them in their marketing and sales endeavors so that their products can be made available on a global scale rather than locally only.

Evolution of Modern-Day Remote Work

At the start of the 20th century, numerous advances led to the establishment of office workspace. The telephone, telegraph, typewriter, and widespread availability of electricity meant that companies could establish office space and hire workers to perform specific job tasks. Public transportation meant that workers were able to travel to and from their homes with relative ease and affordability. Women also entered the workforce at that point to fill the role of secretary, trading the home for the office. Work became associated with commuting to a specific location.

Many women, however, continued to work from home—cooking, sewing, washing, or providing caregiving services such as babysitting. When World War II upended the balance of home–work life, women left home to work in the factories and shipyards to take the places of the men who were fighting the war. The number of women in the workforce grew from 11 million to nearly 20 million between 1941 and 1945. Many of these women returned home at the end of the war; however, they had succeeded in changing the workplace landscape in the United States.

As with many major events throughout history, World War II brought innovations, one of which was technology. The world's first electronic digital computer was built at Iowa State University in 1942. This device helped the military crack enemy codes and laid the groundwork for the telecommuting movement yet to come.

Once women returned to their homes following World War II, they still had the knowledge, skills, and desire to work outside the home. However, they had to find—or make—their own opportunities and most of these involved new types of work-from-home jobs. One of the first opportunities to present itself involved multilevel marketing, such as Tupperware. Housewives were invited to demonstrate Earl Tupper's line of plastic containers at sales parties in their homes. In 1954, Kiplinger's Personal Finance reported that 20 million American women a year attended those sales parties.

Despite the work-from-home multilevel marketing opportunities, by the 1960s, the workforce was predominantly made up of commuters. Most of the work involved physical labor, and manufacturing and textile were the major industries of the day. The small percentage of people who continued to work from home were those involved in creative professions, such as artists and writers.

The 1970s brought several issues that created a need for a different approach to work:

- The Clean Air Act (passed in 1970)
- The OPEC oil embargo (began in 1973)
- "Gridlock" was coined to describe the commuter traffic into and out of cities each day

The Clean Air Act of 1970 authorized the development of comprehensive federal and state regulations to limit emissions from both industrial and mobile sources. Among other provisions, the law required leaded gasoline to be phased out by the mid-1980s. The adoption of this Act occurred at the same time as that of the National Environmental Policy Act that established the U.S. Environmental Protection Agency (EPA). The Clean Air Act was amended in 1977 and again in 1990. The cost of automobiles and other gas-powered vehicles increased significantly as manufacturers struggled to meet new environmental guidelines.

The OPEC oil embargo had a profound impact on the United States and its workers. This embargo ceased oil imports to the United States from participating OPEC nations and began a series of production cuts that altered the price of oil worldwide. These cuts took the price of oil from $2.90 a barrel before the embargo to $11.65 a barrel in January 1974. Gasoline became difficult to obtain. People were forced to wait in long lines at gas stations, and commuters were often concerned about getting to their workplaces. Many people traded larger, gas-guzzling vehicle for smaller, energy-efficient cars and began moderating their use of hot water, heat, and air conditioning in their homes.

The term gridlock first appeared in an IEEE publication in 1971; however, the term was used in a different context in that article than what Sam Schwartz, then chief traffic engineer for the New York City Department of Transportation, meant when he first used the term in the early 1970s. Schwartz revealed that he used the word gridlock internally in his department as early as 1971, recalling that he conceived the term because of a colleague's statement that a proposal to close Broadway to vehicular traffic would simply "lock up the grid." Newspapers first used gridlock in their reports on the 1980 New York City transit strike when all city subway and bus workers walked off their jobs for over a week. The term caught on and eventually was defined by Merriam-Webster as "a traffic jam in which a grid of intersecting streets is so completely congested that no vehicular movement is possible."

Because of these three trends in the early 1970s, people began looking for ways to work that did not require commuting to a specific location. A September 1979 article in *The Washington Post* suggested that working at home could save gasoline. The author of that publication, Frank W. Schiff, did not mean that employees should work from home every day of the week but suggested one or two days a week perhaps. The idea was based on how the potential reduction in volume of travel could impact gasoline consumption, pollution, and gridlock. Schiff explained how working from home could be handled effectively because of the shift in jobs from manufacturing to service and information-related activities. He also discussed the new technologies available in the workplace and how the portability of devices makes working from home much easier. Schiff believed that working from home could be one way to help solve some of our country's persistent problems, and he asked readers to give it a try.

So, in a 1979 experiment conducted by IBM, five employees were allowed to work from home. That experiment set the stage for the growth of remote work so that by 1983, 2,000 employees were working from home. Modern-day remote work policies were eventually adopted by companies by the late 1990s.

While we currently refer to the home-based method of working as remote, the term telecommuting was coined by Jack Nilles, a NASA engineer in 1973 to refer to the act of working from home. People began to branch out and to form start-ups in their homes. These entrepreneurs used their home garages as their headquarters until they could afford to secure an office location elsewhere. Due to the growth in the number of telecommuters by 2000, employers and employees both realized that remote work guidelines were needed. So, the Department of Transportation Appropriations Act was passed. This Act moved remote work into a legitimate category and required employers to provide telecommuting policies.

By 1987, approximately 1.5 million Americans enjoyed telecommuting. That number grew to approximately 10 million by 1990. Approximately 300 companies nationwide successfully employed some type of telecommuters at that time, largely based on their flexibility and a focus on the individuals involved.

In the 1990s, the U.S. Office of Personnel Management and the General Services Administration engaged in the Federal Flexible Workplace Pilot Project. The purpose of this project was to examine the pros and cons of allowing employees to work at locations other than their government office. The nonoffice locations were designated *flexiplaces*. With 550 employees participating in the project, the results were heavily in favor of the pro side of working in nonoffice location. Benefits included the following:

- Improved productivity
- Lowered costs
- Reduced need for office space

After reviewing the findings from the Federal Flexible Workplace Pilot Project, Congress voted for legislation to provide funding for flexiplace work-related equipment and utilities in federal employees' homes. In 1995, the legislation was made permanent.

Former president Bill Clinton issued a Presidential Memorandum in both 1994 and 1995 directing executive branch agencies to create more opportunities for flexible work arrangements. In 1997, the Government Accountability Office (GAO) issued a report that revealed the benefits of telecommuting:

- Reduced commuting time
- Lowered personal costs for expenses of transportation, food, parking, and clothing
- Improved quality of work life and morale
- Improved family–work balance

The United States Census Bureau reported that remote work was on the rise, and that between 2000 and 2010, people who worked from home at least one day per week had risen by over four million to 35 percent of the workforce. The 2013 report stated that in 2010 alone, 13.4 million people worked at home on at least one day per week.

In 2010, former president Barack Obama signed the Telework Enhancement Act. This Act required all federal executive agencies to establish policies to allow eligible employees to work remotely. Between 2014 and 2015, telework participation increased from 39 percent to 46 percent of eligible employees. When asked to provide outcomes from the telework participation, participating agencies cited the following:

- Better emergency preparedness (59 percent)
- Improvement in employee attitudes (58 percent)
- Better opportunities for recruitment (35 percent)
- Better levels of retention (35 percent)
- Reduction in commuter miles for employees (29 percent)
- Improvement in overall employee performance (17 percent)
- Reduction in office expenses and associated costs (17 percent)
- Reduction in amount of energy used (13 percent)

While the reported information dealt strictly with governmental agencies, the increase in remote work was not limited solely to the federal government. In fact, between 2005 and 2015, people engaged in telecommuting at least half-time or more increased by 115 percent. In 2016, the number of people occasionally working from home increased to 43 percent from the previous 37 percent reported in 2015.

In the midst of all of these studies and reports on the usefulness and acceptance of remote work, Vicky Gan and CityLab wrote an article for the December 3, 2015 issue of *The Atlantic* in which they discussed the current U.S. Census numbers reflecting the percentage of Americans working from home and how that number had increased since the founding document on telecommuting was published in 1973. In their estimation, *The Telecommunications-Transportation Tradeoff*, authored by Jack Nilles, F. Roy Carlson, Jr., Paul Gray, and Erhard J. Hanneman, was considered the definitive source for all things telecommuting related. Nilles and his coauthors had proposed telecommuting as an alternative means of managing traffic, sprawl, and the scarcity of nonrenewable resources. As mentioned earlier in this chapter, Nilles is credited with using the term *gridlock* to warn of impending problems with traffic in larger metropolitan cities.

Nilles and his team suggested that either the jobs that employees performed needed to be redesigned so that they could be performed at individual locations or that some type of sophisticated telecommunications and information storage system needed to be developed that would allow the transfer of information to occur between individual locations and the company offices as if employees were all centrally located. Obviously with the invention of the personal computer and the World Wide Web/Internet, these necessary changes took place.

While Nilles and his colleagues knew or hypothesized that technology would not be the limiting factor in the telecommuting process, they likely did not foresee the issues that might arise with job instability and court battles over workers' rights. They also probably could not have forecast the development of the *gig* economy. Flexjobs defined the gig economy as nontraditional work arrangements involving short-term, temporary, or independent contractors—sometimes referred to as a *side hustle*. However, the gig economy or side hustle approach to work is not new. In fact, Nilles and his coauthors likely understood the process; they just called it by a different name. In May 2017, according to the Bureau of Labor Statistics, approximately 10.6 million independent contractors (or 6.9 percent of all

U.S. workers) were gig workers. Less than half of those relied solely on gig work, though, as their sole source (or primary source) of income.

Forty years after the publication of their seminal work on telecommuting, Nilles and his coauthors are still remembered for their informative examination and projections for future consideration. The following quote cannot be paraphrased or reworded as it rings true today as much as it did in 1973:

> We are at a decision point as a society; we must decide whether the way of life made possible by the automobile since the turn of the century will (or can) continue, or if we should consider alternate or modified modes of working, communicating, and living.

Today's Virtual Workplace

The previous section discussed the development and growth of telecommuting and remote work and explored the reasons behind its acceptance and the benefits associated with its use. In this portion of the chapter, we want to look at where we stand currently in the continued development and growth of remote work and the virtual work environment.

No one could have predicted that a singular event would change the work landscape as drastically as that of the 2020 COVID-19 pandemic. This global pandemic brought workplace culture changes that were previously unseen. Andrew Hunter, cofounder of job search engine Adzuna and a Forbes Human Resources Council member, wrote an article for *Forbes* in 2021 describing five ways in which the pandemic changed the U.S. jobs landscape forever:

1. **Redistribution of Opportunities**. Some industries were almost completely wiped out, while others saw accelerated growth. The logistics and warehouse sector grew because of the rise in e-commerce and online deliveries. Jobs in this sector were up by 296 percent in June 2021 compared to prepandemic levels in January 2020. Ultra-low interest rates, home buying, and home improvements increased substantially, thereby driving the demand for laborers and trades professionals up as well. Trade and construction jobs rose by

110 percent in June 2021 as compared to January 2020. However, if you look at the negative side of the pandemic results, various industries including salons, bars, restaurants, and airlines suffered. Service industry jobs such as public relations, advertising, and accounting also suffered and had to cut costs and tighten budgets.

2. **A Focus on Skills Over Formal Education**. A shift in hiring has occurred in that employers are looking for job seekers with particular skills rather than formal education. Data from June 2021 revealed 2.4 million job vacancies open to individuals without college degrees. This opportunity for skilling and reskilling U.S. workers is one that will continue and likely develop further in the next few years. Companies that offer on-the-job training can widen their applicant pools. The resulting impact is a trend toward inclusivity and away from bias favoring education and degrees.

3. **Accelerated Digital Transformation**. Digital skills are at the top of the list for talent desired by employers. Many tech stocks had drastically increased value in the 2020 to 2021 period. Tech also seemed to recover faster than other sectors, such as financial services and consultancy, and accelerated digital transformation did not apply to just tech companies. Teleworking and digitization of health care, retail, and sales meant many different types of companies needed more workers with digital skills. Areas such as digital marketing, social media, data science, and cybersecurity have also seen a growth in demand for workers. Workers need only have the digital know-how, not the relevant college degree, for these types of jobs.

4. **The Rise of Hybrid**. By looking at big tech companies, you can get an idea of where the future of the office is headed—toward hybrid work. Workers who enjoyed the flexibility of working from home during the pandemic resisted the move back to the office, and many organizations found that productivity as good, if not better, when employees worked remotely. As a result, many companies are implementing work-from-anywhere policies; some are going with a work-from-home-forever strategy. However, some challenges must be addressed, such as how to work with employees across multiple or changing time zones, how to adjust pay to fit changing costs of living, how to train and onboard employees remotely, and then the

real heart of the matter—how to manage the changing role of the office itself.

5. **Different Work Benefits**. Many companies began offering work perks—something extra offered to employees beyond wages. These perks are also known as fringe benefits, bonuses, advantages, and more. Employees are demanding more, not necessarily free food or laundry services, but a greater focus on things such as health and well-being and funds that will help them work effectively from home. Many employees want more support for dealing with child care. This issue was brought front and center during the pandemic because of school closures and enforced periods of working from home. Approximately 50 million Americans, one-third of the working population, had a child under 14 in their home at the time of the pandemic. Some companies responded to the child care need during the pandemic by providing onsite day care or backup child care.

As the COVID-19 pandemic raged across the globe in 2020, businesses across the United States closed their doors and upended the lives of their employees. For many, this time away from the workplace was an opportunity to do some soul-searching and to reassess their priorities and their relationships, including with their jobs. Once businesses began to reopen, many employees quit their jobs or demanded that they be allowed to continue working from home or in a hybrid format. Some decided to move to another state or city, some to switch careers entirely, and for some, the pandemic helped them to redefine what work is to them.

During the first months of the COVID-19 quarantine, people hung on to their jobs, even if they hated them. Some workers had to continue going to work at stores, on deliveries, and in factories, even at great risk to themselves and their families. Still others worked from home, literally blurring the lines between work and home.

Women were most negatively affected by the pandemic quarantine and lockdown as they were thrown into child care and homeschooling tasks and simply dropped out of the workforce. Almost 4.2 million women left the job market between February 2020 and April 2020, losing approximately $800 billion in income in 2020.

Despite assertions to the contrary, remote workers were not less engaged during the pandemic lockdown. A study by Harvard Business School revealed that employees spent an average of 48 minutes more per day engaged in work after the lockdown started than they did prepandemic. According to Joanne Lipman, in the June 1, 2021 *Time* article, Americans want remote work, at least part of the time. The ideal would be three days in the office and two days in a remote location. Lipman's assertion is that companies have an unprecedented opportunity for a "redo" on corporate culture. She stated that abandoning the 9-to-5, five-day workweek could be a good start. Also, removing the commute would be another positive for most organizations. Lipman suggested neighborhood co-working hubs or satellite offices. She also recommended that restaurants consider converting dining space into co-working spaces during off hours or offering private rooms for rent by the day for meetings and brainstorming sessions.

However, as we have learned from the postpandemic shutdown, some things are harder to change than others. Not all companies are interested in offering remote work to their employees. Some cite the shortcomings of working from a remote location, such as lack of camaraderie and mentoring, lack of engagement with the company and co-workers, inability to adequately assess work productivity, ineffectiveness for employees who want to be recognized or promoted, and inability to balance home and work. Critics of a remote workforce say it would create a two-tier system of employees—one for those who work onsite and one for remote workers. Those employees who work onsite would be favored over remote workers.

In spite of the potential downsides, Alexandre Judes, Pawel Adrjan, and Tara Sinclair found that the pandemic had essentially created a surge in remote work worldwide. The authors analyzed job postings across 20 countries and determined that the average number of postings, including remote work, had more than tripled. Of course, one argument for this increase was the pandemic restrictions that required business shutdowns and limited movement. Nonetheless, when the pandemic restrictions were eased and people were able to return to work, the average number of postings that included remote work remained near the 7.9 percent peak. Based on the authors' analysis, they concluded that remote work would most likely be more common after the pandemic than before it.

Jon Kennard's article in Unleash included remote working trends to watch for in 2023 and beyond:

- **The capability to work remotely is now expected**. Robert Half, a global recruitment firm, found that 50 percent of professionals who began working from home during the pandemic would leave their jobs if they were forced to return to the workplace on a full-time basis. If not offered remote work, 35 percent of employees would change jobs to one where full-time remote work was available.
- **Remote working productivity remains high**. Employees who work remotely save time and money because they do not have a commute. Employers offer extra benefits to employees through remote work because of these time and money savings; perks workers gain without costing the employers.
- **Remote opportunities continue to grow**. The percentage of companies offering remote work continues to grow. In the United Kingdom, 80 percent of company managers allowed some form of remote work since 2020.
- **With more competition, you get more opportunities**. People are no longer limited by geographic location; they have a world of opportunities available. They can search for their ideal remote job anywhere. Employers gain from this trend also as they can hire the best employees available. Competition works to benefit both employers and employees.
- **Remote work opportunities lead to a broader societal shift**. When high-profile employees are no longer required to live in a specific city to find the world's most competitive jobs, they can take their skillsets anywhere—small towns, rural areas—and bring an added wealth to the economy for those regions that have historically had less. Also, employees who work remotely are found to be happier, on average, than those who work in the office. Job satisfaction and happiness generally should rise as remote work becomes more mainstream.
- **Organizations must make a higher investment in corporate cybersecurity**. For all its advantages, remote work is a

significant threat to data security, revealing that the human–
machine interface is an easy access point. Employees can
be easily manipulated to open e-mail attachments through
emotional manipulation and social engineering. According to
Microsoft, the United States was the target of 46 percent of
cyberattacks in 2020 (double that of any other country).

- **A strong hiring strategy is more important than ever**.
  Companies must use sophisticated systems to appeal to the
  correct market when advertising remote work availabilities.

- **Companies must create an iron-clad remote working
  policy**. These policies are very important in minimizing any
  risks and should be in place before they are really needed.
  Remote working policies should outline expectations and
  protocols. Companies do not want to expose themselves or
  their employees to any unnecessary risks. An effective remote
  working policy also helps a company work toward achieving
  its business goals.

- **Companies need increased knowledge around employee
  tax and legalities**. If companies hire employees from across
  the globe, they must be aware of the complexities and
  legalities involved in the locations where the employees are
  working. In addition, employers must be mindful of varying
  cultural differences regarding work hours, workdays, holidays,
  and daily practices of breaks.

Kennard concluded by hypothesizing that remote and hybrid work
was a definite part of our employment fabric and would continue as the
appetite for it seems to be growing for both employees and employers.

So, despite the cautionary warnings of Lipman, corporations, businesses, and institutions appear to have embraced the remote work model
and have thus far found few legitimate reasons for disrupting the work-
flow. In fact, when asked their biggest concern regarding remote work,
business leaders responded that maintaining the corporate culture was
their number one issue (30 percent).

The information shared in this chapter builds a framework for the
how and why of virtual workplaces—whether we call the arrangement

telecommuting, remote work, working from home, or working from remote locations. Remote work is popular and continues to flourish. The one area not mentioned in any of the research reported for this chapter is that of civility. No one mentioned the potential concerns associated with employees being isolated from onsite offices and losing the ability to communicate interpersonally or the potential for e-mails, instant messages, or other forms of written communication to be misunderstood and result in an act of incivility, or whether working from a remote location would encourage an employee to be less civil in any engagement with the organization due to being "invisible" to co-workers. These questions remain and need to be addressed.

While history teaches us something about how things came to be, we also must examine history to find out where things went wrong. In the next chapter, we will do just that by looking at when and where acts of incivility arose in virtual environments. Our discussion will not be limited to the workplace as defined by a brick-and-mortar building. We will also consider the remote work environment. In addressing the issue, we will hopefully answer the question of whether remote work contributes to the rise in incivility in the virtual environment.

References

"Evolution of the Clean Air Act." November 28, 2022. *United States Environmental Protection Agency*. www.epa.gov/clean-air-act-overview/evolution-clean-air-act#:~:text=The%20enactment%20of%20the%20Clean,industrial)%20sources%20and%20mobile%20sources.

"How Did Gridlock Move So Quickly?" 2022. *Merriam Webster Word History*. www.merriam-webster.com/words-at-play/the-history-of-gridlock.

"How Do We Know? Working at Home Is on the Rise." June 3, 2013. *United States Census Bureau*. www.census.gov/library/visualizations/2013/comm/home_based_workers.html.

"Remote Work Statistics in 2022 and How They Will Influence the Workplace in 2023." December 6, 2022. *Squaretalk*. https://squaretalk.com/remote-work-statistics/.

Gan, V. and CityLab. December 3, 2015. "What Telecommuting Looked Like in 1973: A Vision of Remote Work Before the Personal Computer." *The Atlantic*. www.theatlantic.com/technology/archive/2015/12/what-telecommuting-looked-like-in-1973/418473/.

Gupta, A. November 2, 2022. "The History of Remote Work: How It Came to Be What It Is Today." *Sorry, I Was on Mute.* www.sorryonmute.com/history-remote-work-industries/.

Hunter, A. June 1, 2021. "Five Ways the Pandemic Has Changed the U.S. Jobs Landscape Forever." *Forbes.* www.forbes.com/sites/forbeshumanresources council/2021/06/01/five-ways-the-pandemic-has-changed-the-us-jobs-landscape-forever/?sh=3024f4364505.

Judes, A., P. Adrjan, and T. Sinclair. December 16, 2021. "Will Remote Work Persist After the Pandemic?" *Hiring Lab.* www.hiringlab.org/2021/12/16/will-remote-work-persist-after-the-pandemic/.

Kennard, J. October 19, 2022. "Nine Remote Working Trends to Look Out for in 2022 and 2023." *Unleash.* www.unleash.ai/future-of-work/remote-working-trends/.

Knobelsdorff, K.E. June 8, 1987. "Telecommuting: Reality Sets in." *The Christian Science Monitor.* www.csmonitor.com/1987/0608/ftelly.html.

Lambert, J. October 25, 2021. "Microsoft Digital Defense Report Shares New Insights on Nation-State Attacks." www.microsoft.com/en-us/security/blog/2021/10/25/microsoft-digital-defense-report-shares-new-insights-on-nation-state-attacks/.

Lipman, J. June 1, 2021. "The Pandemic Revealed How Much We Hate Our Jobs. Now We Have a Chance to Reinvent Work." *Time.* https://time.com/6051955/work-after-covid-19/.

Madell, R. 2022. "Gig Economy." *Flexjobs.* www.flexjobs.com/blog/post/what-is-the-gig-economy-v2/?gclid=EAIaIQobChMInM6A_pCB_AIVGIvICh3bk AwBEAAYAyAAEgIwO_D_BwE.

Nilles, J.M., F.R. Carlson, Jr., P. Gray, and G.J. Hanneman. 2007. *The Telecommunications-Transportation Tradeoff: Options for Tomorrow.* ISBN 13: 978-1419667299.

O'Donnellan, R. January 4, 2022. "Remote Working Statistics You Need to Know in 2022." *Intuition.* www.intuition.com/remote-working-statistics-you-need-to-know-in-2022/#content.

Reynolds, B.W. and B. Adrianne. 2022. *The Complete History of Working From Home.* www.flexjobs.com/blog/post/complete-history-of-working-from-home/.

Schiff, F.W. September 2, 1979. "Working at Home Can Save Gasoline." *The Washington Post.* www.washingtonpost.com/archive/opinions/1979/09/02/working-at-home-can-save-gasoline/ffa475c7-d1a8-476e-8411-8cb53f1f34 70/?utm_term=.f4f061b67f21.

CHAPTER 5

Incivility

The "Nasty" Side of the Virtual Environment

The World Wide Web was once thought to have the greatest potential for connecting people across nations, political divides, ethnicities, genders, generations, and more. The ability to connect with others and to build communities of like-minded individuals held great promise. Inclusivity and constructive discussion were buzzwords for the new era. As the years have unfolded, however, we have seen increasing concern that the Internet has led to a deterioration in the quality of interactivity driven in part by incivility, hate speech, and trolling.

Robert Putnam warned of the decline in social engagement in his book *Bowling Alone*. Participation in formal organizations, informal social connectedness, and interpersonal trust issues were prevalent in the United States in the 1960s and 1970s. Putnam's reference to interpersonal trust referred to an individual's expectation that any statements or promises made by another could be relied upon regardless of that individual's familiarity or relationship with that other person.

Moreover, these measures of social capital began a rapid decline in the 1980s and 1990s. Others who followed Putnam noted a decline in volunteerism, membership in organizations, and entertainment with friends and family. In fact, a trend emerged in the decline of social connectedness and confidence in institutions in the United States between 1975 and 2002. Putnam discussed three reasons for the decline in American social capital:

1. The reduction in time available for social activities because of the need to work more and to spend commuting to and from the workplace.

2. The rise in mobility of workers.
3. The growth in technology and mass media.

Other researchers validated Putnam's reasoning, adding layers to his statements, particularly regarding the reduction in time available for social engagement. The unfriendly environment for social engagement had prompted the substitution of materialistic values. So, by substituting rewards of goods, social isolation became increasingly preferred. Individuals chose to watch a movie alone through their home theatre system rather than go to the local cinema with friends. Because of their social isolation and the desire for more and more goods, people devoted themselves to work.

Putnam argued that the growth in the use of technology would only serve to further isolate people. As we look at the number of social networking sites and the volume of e-mails and messages sent and received, we can see reason for Putnam's claim. At its core, communication takes place between two people, a sender of the message and a receiver of the message (audience). When people use technology (e.g., the computer, mobile phone, or tablet), the technology becomes the receiver or audience of the message. Because technology is inanimate, no personal feelings or reactions are involved in the communication process. So, the message is depersonalized, and the writer becomes less self-aware, thus the content can become less than civil.

When people engage in incivility online, they decrease others' willingness to participate in discussions. They serve to silence minority perspectives and produce environments in which people avoid expressing their opinions. In fact, online or virtual environments have the potential to train people to accept that certain behaviors are normal, including acts of incivility. Those who see and read these posts or messages may even adopt similar verbally aggressive behaviors themselves.

The virtual environment provides opportunities for anonymous interactions. People do not have to reveal their actual names or images. They can adopt avatars to depict themselves and choose pseudonyms instead of displaying their real names. No one forces them to display their legal information. After all, part of the draw to the environment has been the lure of anonymity. While the dark side of anonymity can take us beyond incivility and into crime and criminal acts outside our moral understanding (e.g., pedophilia, human trafficking, stalking), for most, engaging in aggressive and disrespectful behaviors, harassment, and other acts of incivility are those most often displayed across virtual platforms.

Acts of incivility are not limited to social media. E-mail rudeness is also a problem that is growing.

E-mail

E-mail incivility can take two forms: active e-mail rudeness and passive e-mail rudeness. Active e-mail rudeness is just what the name says—a nasty message. Passive e-mail rudeness involves the act of ignoring a co-worker's e-mail request despite the co-worker's need for a response before being able to move forward with a work project.

Following the COVID-19 pandemic, when so many people were working remotely, e-mail became the official communication channel for companies. As early as 2009, a study of professionals reported that more than 90 percent had experienced disrespectful, uncivil e-mail exchanges at work.

In 2020, Zhenyu Yuan conducted research into e-mail incivility. One of the requests Yuan made of people was to provide examples of rude e-mails they received. Based on a review of the e-mails, Yuan concluded that e-mail incivility is a problem that many people are experiencing in their workplaces and that e-mail incivility creates a stressful environment for employees.

In a study published in 2020, Kimberly McCarthy, Jone L. Pearce, John Morton, and Sarah Lyon looked at the potential consequences of cyber incivility, a phrase they used to describe e-mail behavior that is perceived by the recipient as disrespectful, insensitive, and a violation of the established norms for mutual respect. The researchers based their study on the prior research findings that revealed (1) incivility in e-mail messages caused daily stress for employees, and (2) the heavier the workload or the higher the pressure in a job, the more likely the employee is to respond with incivility. McCarthy and her fellow researchers reported that face-to-face incivility had previously been studied and had been shown to threaten the well-being of organizations; nonetheless, they believed that knowledge of computer-generated forms of incivility was limited and needed further study due to the increase in technology use and the potential harm that could arise from unchecked acts of incivility. Based on the work that McCarthy and her coresearchers completed, they were able to report the following:

- Being exposed to rude e-mail behavior decreased employees' performance on subsequent tasks.
- Exposure to a rude e-mail has a greater negative impact on an employee's subsequent task performance than being exposed to rude face-to-face behavior.
- Exposure to rudeness—in whatever venue (face-to-face or via e-mail)—is contagious and can result in performance issues for uninvolved third parties.

Following on the theme established by McCarthy and her coresearchers, an article in *Scientific American* looked at the psychological toll of rude e-mails. The authors, Zhenyu Yuan and YoungAh Park, asked readers to consider the impact of receiving an e-mail on a Monday morning that had been typed entirely in all capital letters—and with exclamation points included. You have just been yelled at by a co-worker before you had your morning coffee. Yet, these types of e-mails happen frequently. Rude e-mails are on the rise according to Yuan and Park. For a society that likes to call itself civilized, we have certainly wandered far away from the norms of society once associated with civility. Rudeness has become the norm today, and it has become a pervasive problem.

While e-mail has made communication more efficient, it also creates a distant and detached style of interacting with others. When we sit in front of a computer screen, we seem to forget decency. If we were meeting with an individual in a face-to-face setting, we would not ignore questions or requests or respond rudely. Yet, with e-mail, we do just that. And for people who are receiving these rude e-mails, they can feel the effects far longer than the time needed to create the message and send it. The stress associated with e-mail incivility can creep into personal and family life because employees who receive messages of this type report feeling more stress symptoms afterward, in the evening and the following morning.

The saddest part of the e-mail incivility issue is that the effect felt by employees receiving these messages spreads, usually to those closest to them—their friends and families. Yuan and Park stated that the effects of one poorly constructed, uncivil message can have a chain reaction. The stress signals spread from employee to family member and so on, especially in dual-income families.

After reading the preceding information on e-mail incivility, I must admit that I am guilty of passive e-mail incivility. I had absolutely no idea that by ignoring an e-mail or delaying a response to a message, I was engaging in an act of incivility. As a college professor, I manage hundreds of students each semester, including the communications that arise from course interactions and follow-ups. In addition to my student population, I also have e-mails from colleagues and professional connections that are making requests or scheduling meetings and require my input. If you add the external e-mail that I also manage—my personal messages from friends and family—then you find an overwhelming stream of daily e-mails.

Quite often, I use the subject line information in an e-mail to determine the level of importance, basing that on whether the sender is asking for information, seeking to schedule a meeting, or providing updates or information. If the subject lines in those messages are vague or nonexistent, then I push them to the bottom of my *to-do* list without reading them. Likely by taking this approach, I am missing some requests for assistance or information that the sender or writer of the message is waiting for me to provide. By gaining a better understanding of passive e-mail incivility, I now am prepared to manage my e-mail and to stress to my students the importance of a subject line that conveys the purpose of the message. They will also benefit by learning about passive e-mail incivility and how that approach can be detrimental to relationships, especially in the workplace.

With the growth in remote working, e-mail rudeness must be addressed. The use of e-mail has opened Pandora's box, but we cannot allow incivility to thrive in our inboxes.

Social Media Networking Sites

Ashley Anderson and Dominique Brossard looked at how uncivil online interactions could contribute to division over an issue. When looking at incivility in posts to social media networking sites (SNS), we must consider what that means. We examined the rise in incivility in e-mails and can easily see how an act of incivility in e-mail—whether passive or active—can impact an individual and others beyond that individual. However, when discussing posts to various social media sites, incivility may take a different approach.

As mentioned earlier in this chapter, social media platforms allow individuals to create pseudonyms and to use avatars or clipart for photos. People use this anonymity to do and say whatever they wish without fear of repercussion (unless they violate the rules of some SNS sites and are temporarily banned for a specific period). So, incivility in this venue can range from rude comments to name-calling. People may also post outrageous claims or engage in flaming (defined as incensed discussion). Incivility on the Internet can result in heated, volatile discussions that fall far short of rational and reasoned conversations.

Anderson and Brossard discussed the side effects of these uncivil posts stating that individuals react negatively to online incivility that is directed toward them or their view. In addition, incivility creates hatred or humiliation responses and influences readers' opinions of the credibility of the author. Probably the worst impact of online incivility occurs when individuals' posts question or target the political or religious beliefs of the writers. The outcome here is that people can be influenced by those negative attitudes about a specific topic or issue.

An interesting finding from the study conducted by Anderson and Brossard is that people's perceptions of topics are shaped in the online environment by both experts who published the information as well as by others' civil or uncivil responses. In fact, they learned that even though the Internet opened doors for SNS and for public discussion of important and current topics, nonexpert—and sometimes rude—individuals are also given a new voice and that voice may be the loudest and the one most remembered by others.

Following the Anderson and Brossard study, Angelo Antoci, Alexia Delfino, Fabio Paglieri, Fabrizio Panebianco, and Fabio Sabatini conducted a study to examine the dark side of online social interactions. Antoci and his colleagues reported that mounting evidence showed online incivility to be spreading across social networking sites, turning them into hostile environments. The Pew Research Center examined the incidence of incivility in SNS interactions and found that 73 percent of individuals in that environment have seen someone being harassed on social networking sites, with 40 percent reporting they had been the recipient of those acts.

Antoci and his coauthors stated that people who interact in the social networking sites condition their own behaviors to match the behavior of others. If they enter a hostile environment where incivility is the dominant communication approach, individuals can decide whether they wish to behave rudely as well or to leave the social network.

Some posts and interactions on social media go beyond rude or disrespectful comments, falling into the hate speech category. Even when social media moderators attempt to squelch one hate group, another simply appears in its place. Physicist and complexity researcher Neil Johnson of George Washington University in Washington, DC, created mathematical models to analyze data involving online hate culture. Johnson believes that hate is a living, evolving organism, and through his analysis, he is attempting to track its spread and interactions over time. His work provides evidence demonstrating how online social media helps individuals unify across platforms and create what he labels *hate bridges* across nations and cultures.

Johnson and his colleagues began their project by defining hate groups as those with users who express animosity toward or advocate for violence against a particular race or social group. Applying this definition and the mathematical algorithm, Johnson identified more than 1,000 hate groups on multiple platforms. The most interesting facet of his research revealed the interactions between related groups. The hate groups did not gather in a single place but rather would meet on different networks. The more closely watched or the tighter the restrictions on a particular platform, the more likely the hate group will be to form cross-platform linkages or *hate highways*.

As content moderation continues to escalate and evolve and the removal of harmful and irrelevant posts grows, hate groups will not simply disappear, though. They change tactics. According to Punyajoy Saha and colleagues, the response from hate groups to these advances in moderations is a newer form of harmful content—fear speech. Fear speech is designed to create and spread fear about a particular target group or community online (and eventually, the real world). This type of fear can cause normal, peace-loving people to become extremists. Social media makes the spread of such fear tactics extremely easy.

If users of social media platforms condition themselves to match their behaviors to those of others on that platform, as mentioned earlier, you can see how the spread of fear speech can grow. Saha and colleagues examined 280,000 users' posts on a loosely moderated social media platform named Gab.com. Gab is a Twitter-like social media platform that was launched in May 2016 and allows posts up to 3,000 characters in length. What Saha and colleagues uncovered in their examination was that 9,200 users posted at least 10 fear or hate speech posts. A follow-up review of Twitter and Facebook by Saha and colleagues revealed these posts cross into other social media platforms as both had hate speech and fear speech postings, albeit better moderated than those on Gab.

A group that disproportionately suffers from the posts of hate groups are teens. These young, impressionable people are targets of these hate groups, and they want them to read and share their posts. They want them to buy into their fear speech—something that goes far beyond incivility and disrespect, as these hate groups desire teenagers to embrace their extremist mentality. Social media has the ability to create and promote violence, especially when we do not use our reputable sources to verify information before responding to or sharing posts.

Recently, I abandoned Twitter because of the uncivil comments and interactions on that social networking site. Previously I had enjoyed reading the information available on Twitter and engaging in online discussions with others. However, as the prevalence of rudeness, crude comments, and hate-filled speech became the norm, I decided I no longer needed to be in that hostile environment. Now I am more active on LinkedIn and spend more time engaging with users on that SNS. I will not say that you cannot occasionally find a rude comment or a post that does not quite "sound" right; but as most of the members of LinkedIn are professionals, the likelihood of incivility becoming the norm is somewhat less.

A report of findings from researchers at the University of Arizona provided another lens through which to view incivility in the virtual or

online environment. In discussing social networking sites and other platforms, the researchers stated that to increase engagement with information, most platforms allowed users to evaluate comments made by others
through a rating system (e.g., Like, Down/Up votes).

The use of these rating systems raised a civility concern about online
behavior regarding discussions. When the researchers examined 6,000
online newspaper comments, they uncovered an interesting occur-
rence: repeated incivility posts (when the initial incivility was affirmed
by both comments and votes) by the same person are more likely to
occur. In addition, the more incivility was expressed in comments, the
more frequently the repeated incivility posts received positive votes. The
researchers explained that readers wanted to see the incivility validated in
responses or comments. If they did, then the posts were more likely to
receive positive affirmation in the form of a *Like* or an *Up Vote*. Therefore,
the researchers concluded that users of SNS sites are more likely to promote incivility when it is affirmed by others (i.e., incivility is included in
comments and responses).

Still other researchers analyzed posts by categorizing incivility as being
either tone-based or content-based. Tone-based incivility is based on the
theory of politeness and includes the following characteristics:

- Use of profanities against an individual or someone
  commenting on the topic, against an idea or institution, or
  against a particular race, religion, gender, or ethnicity.
- Use of all capital letters to indicate yelling or shouting.
- Use of personal insults against a person or someone
  commenting on the topic.
- Use of unrelated information outside of the topic.

Content-based incivility, on the other hand, refers to the meaning of
the message itself. Posts using content-based incivility may not contain
any derogatory language, vulgarities, or use of racial slurs. Instead, content-based incivility contains the following:

- Stereotyping a group using "isms" or certain political beliefs.
- Stereotyping an individual or group using racial epithets.

- Threatening a group's rights.
- Asserting supremacy based on racial, ethnic, religious, geographic, sexual, and gender orientation.
- Sharing false information without providing facts.
- Making an emotional appeal to harm a specific group or person either psychologically, emotionally, financially, or otherwise.

One of the main reasons for characterizing incivility as either tone-based or content-based is related to technology itself. Tone-based uncivil messages can be handled with technological interventions that many social media companies, news organizations, and others already use. The content-based uncivil messages, however, pose a greater level of difficulty in managing due to their very nature.

Regardless of how incivility is categorized, its rise in the virtual environment continues. We appear to be cursing more, taking longer to answer e-mails (or not responding at all), failing to follow-up on important tasks, preferring to be socially isolated, and essentially losing all our interpersonal skills. We are breaking up via e-mail; butchering the English language in our online posts, our e-mails, and text messages; failing to send thank-you messages or notes; and, in general, burying our heads in the sand until an uncivil post or e-mail demands our attention.

Our clients are following suit. They are ghosting us. Ghosting is defined *Merriam-Webster* as the act of abruptly cutting off contact with someone (or an organization) without any explanation or by avoiding/refusing to answer any phone calls, e-mails, or instant messages. Ghosting is an act of incivility, a passive form, sure, but one that has ramifications beyond the incivility itself.

Addressing incivility and attempting to control its impact is important to the overall physical and psychological well-being of everyone. In a democratic society, we should be able to engage in civil conversations. If people engage in uncivil discourse, they will continue to affect those discussions. Corporations, organizations, institutions, and companies also benefit from an engaged society. People share ideas, and those ideas often develop into products and services. If fear of attacks on social media sites and other platforms prevents people from interacting, we have lost multiple opportunities for growth and exploration.

Online Learning/Training, Meeting, and Presentations

Uncivil behavior in the teaching and learning environment is not new. The only difference now is the venue in which these incidences of uncivil behavior occur—the online or virtual environment.

The transition from face-to-face classes to online has not been an easy one for many. Students are often unfamiliar with how to learn in an online class and approach courses with a great deal of fear and concern. Still others believe that online classes are easier than face-to-face and require little to no effort in completing.

When the COVID-19 pandemic forced colleges and universities to close their doors and send students home to complete courses by remote instruction, all students got to experience the online learning environment first hand, those with experience and those who had never considered taking an online class.

Suddenly, students were learning about synchronous delivery of classes, and they quickly became well-versed in the use of Zoom for online class meetings and Microsoft Teams for scheduling meetings with faculty. These virtual platforms were largely responsible for all interactions between an instructor and students in that instructor's class. I was one of those instructors.

Having familiarity with online meeting platforms, I quickly adapted to using Zoom for class meetings. However, I noticed that my students were frequently engaging in uncivil behavior. Now, I admit that for many, they had little to no training in the use of Zoom or Microsoft Teams. They were essentially "winging it" and attempting to get through the course, just as many other students around the globe were doing. Students would present to the class at the start time (or thereafter depending on their time management skills) with their web cameras on and their microphones muted. I would check with everyone at the beginning to ensure they could hear my voice and see everyone on the screen. Once I began the discussion, I noticed something happening—cameras were being turned off. The list of participants indicated the students were still in the Zoom class, but I could not see them to verify that information. This type of behavior showed a lack of respect for me and was rude. If we had been in the face-to-face classroom, these students would have had no choice but to remain in the room or simply not attend class on that day.

Other students did not participate in any of the discussions. They were visible on the screen; however, they simply did not respond to anything. They drank coffee, ate food (sometimes messily), sat (or laid) in their beds with the covers pulled up, slept while sitting up and on camera, walked in and out of the camera view, played with their dogs or cats on screen, and essentially tuned me out. But they were present in the class for purposes of physical attendance.

Students were unaware of the proper placement of their laptop or mobile device so that the web camera would be positioned to show their face and upper shoulders in the screen. Often, I found myself looking up their noses as the laptop was in their laps. On occasion, I (and their classmates) was treated to a view of lingerie. Roommates or family members wandered in and out of the camera view, sometimes waving.

I attempted to be understanding as we were all under a great deal of stress, dealing with a pandemic that had no cure, as well as external factors such as family responsibilities and unemployment. So, to help deal with some of the issues, I created a presentation on proper behaviors in a virtual learning environment. I explained the placement of the web camera, the use of a green screen to block the view of the room where they were located during the class sessions, the most appropriate attire for a synchronous class meeting, tips on eating and drinking during a synchronous meeting, and a few other important points that I believed useful for my class as well as the other classes they were also taking.

Despite my best intentions, students' behaviors did not change. As time passed, students began using e-mail to send uncivil messages demanding that I change something or alter a grade with the threat of going to the dean or the president of the university to file a complaint. In none of these instances had I done anything differently from what I normally did. The students knew the rules for the course as they were spelled out in the syllabus. However, because of its conversion to the virtual environment, students believed the course should change—or that I should change—to better serve them. After all, they pay my salary. They should be able to tell me what they want, and I should deliver it.

Now, you may think that many of the behaviors mentioned earlier do not rise to the level of incivility. However, these acts reflect the disinhibition effect of online presence. Scientists call the disinhibition effect the perception of anonymity that allows a person to act in ways that they would not in a face-to-face setting because they see no personal cost involved. Being unafraid of any consequences leads to risky behaviors, thereby jeopardizing themselves and other students enrolled in the course with them.

While the training venue differs somewhat from the online educational environment, mostly because training courses typically do not involve grades, it still faces many of the same struggles. With online training, particularly if delivered synchronously, a key concern for incivility would be topics for discussion and how responses might affect participants' engagement. Despite the statement earlier that most people are more prone to write uncivil comments in e-mails, texts, and so on, training courses present a different perspective regarding the learners involved and whether they chose the training session, or it was required of them. If the topic of the training is one that impacts individuals' belief systems, you may find the discussion takes on an air of incivility when participants start saying they do not agree with something, or that something that has been said is incorrect. You need only one trainee to begin the process of uncivil comments before others feel emboldened to join.

Of course, when training takes place onsite, trainers have the benefit of observation. They can determine from the body language of trainees what emerging issues are coming. Trainers observe these cues to anticipate any support requirements necessary to ensure a productive training session. However, once training moves to the virtual environment, trainers lose that contact and must find alternatives to encourage trainees to remain on task and involved in the learning process.

Even as trainers have had to learn how to navigate new technologies, retool their resources, repurpose existing activities, and concentrate on ensuring that their timing is right, they also have discovered an entirely new group of trainee behaviors that require unique solutions.

Marc Ratcliffe, in an article in *Talent Development (TD)*, discussed this variety of new learner behaviors that have arisen with virtual training and classified them according to descriptive character names:

- **Gaslighters**. When discussing personal relationships, the term gaslighting is often used to describe manipulation and emotional abuse. When using it in the virtual training environment, we are talking about individual learners/trainees who demonstrate similar traits. They attempt to create a false narrative that causes other learners/trainees to question their own understanding, to second-guess their decisions, and to invalidate their contributions. This behavior causes other learners/trainees to stop speaking (both literally and figuratively) because they cease all involvement and engagement.

- **Ghosts**. These learners/trainees are disengaged. They keep their cameras off, their microphones on mute, and do not participate in any polls or chat box interactions. They are logged in. That is all.

- **Influencers**. Just as on social media, influencers can sway an audience for either positive or negative responses. Some influencers want to do good things; others are focused on their own self-interests. When engaging in virtual training, the influencers who are in it for themselves focus on their own issues regardless of the group's needs. They hijack the content and marginalize other learners/trainees.

- **Keyboard Warriors**. These learners/trainees are aggressive and are characterized by abusive or dismissive comments. They can create a toxic learning environment and usually make anonymous contributions under the use of a pseudonym or some other concealed identity. Keyboard Warriors believe they can act however they wish without any fear of punishment.

- **Multitaskers**. These learners/trainees are the ones who believe they can complete multiple jobs while also engaging in virtual training. They will have dozens of tabs open on their computer, with numerous pop-up notifications and alerts appearing during the training session. How much content are these learners/trainees really acquiring?

- **Noobs**. Ed Boon coined this term as a short form for *newbie* in the Mortal Kombat game, and it quickly caught on in the gamer world. However, for purposes of virtual training, noob describes a person who is a novice user and unfamiliar with the virtual learning platform. These individuals can become easily frustrated, so they can often completely derail the learning session. Noobs need assistance troubleshooting technical issues, and more time gets devoted to working through those problems than on the content of the training. Other learners/trainees are negatively affected by a noob's technical issues.

- **Technophobes**. Unlike noobs who will eventually develop skills and improve with practice, technophobes have a disdain for technology as well as a fundamental fear of it. They often practice avoidance techniques rather than seek improvement opportunities. Technophobes' anxiety negatively impacts their ability to process and retain information.

- **Zoombies**. These trainees are the individuals who regularly attend back-to-back virtual meetings and videoconferences. They have lower energy levels and are less motivated. They also have difficulty with concentration.

These characters and learner behaviors can also be found in online courses, virtual meetings, and audioconferences. However, organizations, educators, and trainers can develop early groundwork for their virtual environment activities and minimize problem behaviors to keep these characters in check.

Uncivil behaviors can occur across a continuum in the virtual environment. They can range from disruption to covert or overt threats. Despite the nature of online courses, meetings, and training sessions, most of the uncivil acts occur via other venues—e-mail, texts, discussions, chats, or group work. This does not mean that acts of incivility cannot be seen in virtual sessions. Incivility can be as subtle as a learner/trainee/participant wearing apparel that communicates a message about a political organization, a campaign, or a protest or that contains offensive language or offensive images. Another subtle way to engage in incivility can simply be the visible artwork or objects behind the learner/trainee/participant. These items can be a red flag to others in the virtual session that can cause them to lose focus on the content because of their intense response to the subtle message.

In the final chapter of this book, we will review strategies to help you ensure that incivility does not become a problem in your virtual environment. We will examine what companies, organizations, institutions, and individuals are currently doing to build a better virtual environment for everyone involved. While incivility may be a fact of life, you and your organization do not have to accept its existence without arming yourself with some tools to battle it and to reduce its influence in your virtual environments.

References

"Findings From University of Arizona Provides New Data on Computers (Social Norms and the Dynamics of Online Incivility)." March 31, 2021. *Computer Weekly News*. Gale General OneFile 255. https://link.gale.com/apps/doc/A656588592/ITOF?u=tel_middleten&sid=ebsco&xid=9cb08b83 (accessed December 18, 2022).

"Ghosting." 2022. *Merriam-Webster*. www.merriam-webster.com/dictionary/ghosting.

Anderson, A.A. and B. Dominique. 2014. "The 'Nasty Effect': Online Incivility and Risk Perceptions of Emerging Technologies." *Journal of Computer-Mediated Communication* 19, pp. 373–387.

Antoci, A., A. Delfino, F. Paglieri, F. Panebianco, and F. Sabatini. November 1, 2016. "Civility Vs. Incivility in Online Social Interactions: An Evolutionary Approach." *PLoS One* 11, no. 11. https://doi.org/10.1371/journal.pone.0164286.

Borchers, C. September 8, 2022. "What the #@$%! Happened to Our Manners at Work?" *Wall Street Journal*. www.wsj.com/articles/what-the-happened-to-our-manners-at-work-11662584091.

Frederick, E. August 22, 2019. "Dark Pools of Hate Flourish Online. Here Are Four Controversial Ways to Fight Them: A New Study Maps the 'Ecology' of Online Hate Groups Across Platforms." *Science*. www.science.org/content/article/dark-pools-hate-flourish-online-here-are-4-controversial-ways-fight-them. https://doi.org/10.1126/science.aaz2320.

Gaskell, M. December 15, 2022. "Reindeer Games: How Educators Can Explain, Reduce Online Bullying." *SmartBrief.* https://corp.smartbrief.com/original/2022/12/reindeer-games-how-educators-can-explain-reduce-online-bullying.

Jayson, S. August 8, 2011. "At Work, No More Mr. Nice Guy." *USA Today.* Gale in Context: Opposing Viewpoints. https://link.gale.com/apps/doc/A253951311/OVIC?u=tel_middleten&sid=ebsco&xid=5174f737 (accessed October 22, 2022).

McCarthy, K., J.L. Pearce, J. Morton, and S. Lyon. 2020. "Do You Pass It On? An Examination of the Consequences of Perceived Cyber Incivility." *Organization Management Journal* 17, no. 1, pp. 43–58.

Miller, S. September 25, 2020. "E-mail Incivility Is a Real Problem: UIC Researchers." *WBBM Newsradio.* www.audacy.com/wbbm780/news/local/email-incivility-is-a-real-problem-study.

NieBen, D. December 17, 2020. "Interpersonal Trust Is Highly Relevant in Society." https://blogs.biomedcentral.com/on-society/2020/12/17/interpersonal-trust-is-highly-relevant-in-society/.

Owens, D.M. February 2012. "Incivility Rising: Researchers Say Workers Might Not Have the Time to Be Civil." *HR Magazine*, p. 33.

Putnam, R.D. 2000. *Bowling Alone: The Collapse and Revival of American Community.* New York, NY: Simon & Schuster.

Ratcliffe, M. February 2022. "Difficult Virtual Learner Conduct Be Gone." *Talent Development (TD)* 76, no. 2, pp. 26–31.

Saha, P., K. Garimella, N.K. Kalyan, S.K. Pandey, P.M. Meher, B. Matthew, and A. Mukherjee. March 6, 2023. "On the Rise of Fear Speech in Online Social Media." *PNAS* 120, p. 11. https://doi.org/10.1073/pnas.2212270120.

Sanyal, S. 2019. "Tone-Based Incivility and Content-Based Incivility: A Framework to Examine Online Uncivil Discourse." *Electronic Thesis Collections*, p. 339. https://digitalcommons.pittstate.edu/etd/339.

Shmargad, Y., K. Coe, K. Kenski, and S.A. Rains. 2022. "Social Norms and the Dynamics of Online Incivility." *Social Science Computer Review* 40, no. 3, pp. 717–735. https://doi.org/10.1177/0894439320985527.

Yuan, Z. and Y. Park. July 21, 2020. "The Psychological Toll of Rude E-mails." *Scientific American.* www.scientificamerican.com/article/the-psychological-toll-of-rude-e-mails/.

CHAPTER 6

Managing Incivility in Virtual Environments

Now that we have reviewed civility and its history and the growth of technology and how incivility permeated that platform, we must address the elephant in the room: If we know incivility exists in the virtual environment, how do we deal with it and its effects on employees, trainees, students, and the people with whom they interact.

The Civility in America 2011 poll of 1,000 adults conducted by Weber Shandwick and Powell Tate, in partnership with KRC Research, revealed that 67 percent of those responding saw a critical need for civility training in the workplace. They believed this was the first step toward managing incivility and restoring respect at work.

In her article in *HR Magazine*, Donna Owens recommended that employers start with screening for personality styles or conflict management styles when recruiting prospective employees. Based on research conducted by Jeannie Trudel and Thomas G. Reio, Jr., individuals with collaborative styles of conflict management are more likely to engage in civil behavior than individuals with a more forceful, aggressive style of conflict management.

Another suggested method for managing incivility is the development and implementation of a policy and code of conduct in the workplace directed toward encouraging respect and acceptable behaviors. In addition, the inclusion of leadership training and role modeling as well as collaborative strategies to help people learn to engage in positive ways are other effective methods for developing a civil workplace. Owens suggested that human resource professionals help employees deal with stress to ensure that it does not accumulate. Also, involving employees in decisions regarding changes is an important component of reducing stress and keeping them informed. Employees who feel involved and informed are less likely to be engaged in incivility in the workplace.

Shelby Joy Scarbrough in her 2020 book *Civility Rules!* devoted a chapter to each of the five core ideals associated with civility: courtesy, humility, empathy, trust, and honor/respect. She believed that we must all follow these societal standards and learn to coexist productively and peacefully; however, to do so requires that we celebrate the uniqueness of individuals and their rights to be independent beings. Scarbrough stated that if we follow these simple principles, we can build a civil society—for free—without a huge time and resource investment. She lamented the potential absence of civility, though, saying that the lack of civility could cost us everything.

One of the principles in Scarbrough's book is that of empathy. The connection between empathy and civility resonates with many people, including radio host and entrepreneur Abhi Golhar. According to Scarbrough, Golhar believes that we can increase our emotional intelligence (EQ) and, thus, empathy by doing the following:

- Employ a direct style of communicating but still be respectful of the feelings of others.
- Respond to conflict; don't react to it. The goal is to come to a resolution so keep your words and actions in alignment with your goal.
- Practice active listening. Stop planning what you want to say and waiting for the chance to respond. Actually listen to the words the person is saying and let that person finish speaking.
- Be self-aware and maintain a positive attitude. If you are aware of the moods and emotional state of others, you can adjust your own attitudes and behaviors accordingly—especially if your attitude is negative.
- Accept criticism with dignity and grace. Try to understand where the criticism is coming from and then work constructively to resolve any issues.
- Empathize with others. The practice of empathy leads to mutual respect. Positive conversations can develop in situations where people feel respected, even when opinions differ.
- Use positive leadership skills to take initiative and make good decisions. Increase your ability to solve problems.

- Develop your interpersonal skills and be approachable and sociable. Strong interpersonal skills help you communicate more effectively.

Navigating the virtual environment is not vastly different in its requirements for practicing civility than the onsite environment, aside from the major difference being the medium for engagement. As we discussed in the chapter on the development of virtual environments, the one sticking point that people have used to their advantage in practicing inappropriate online behavior is anonymity. For many, the ability to post to social media platforms using an avatar and a fake name emboldens them to write bullying, hostile, and sometimes even threatening posts—all under the guise of free speech.

Numerous organizations, states, and institutions have implemented civility policies. One example is that of the Department of Human Resource Management for the State of Virginia that implemented Policy 2.35 Civility in the workplace. As part of the document, the department included a glossary of terms to help employees fully understand what constituted specific acts of incivility. The term cyberbullying was defined as follows:

Using technology to intentionally harm others through hostile behavior, threatening, disrespectful, demeaning, or intimidating messages. Bullying that occurs via the Internet, cell phones, or other devices (e-mails, IMs, text messages, blogs, pictures, videos, postings on social media, etc.). Pretending to be the victim or spreading rumors or visual images online in order to denigrate or marginalize the targeted person.

The Human Resource Department specifically included cyberbullying along with bullying as two important terms in its policy. The goal for Virginia state agencies, as specified in this policy, is to ensure that employees, customers, clients, contract workers, volunteers, and other third parties have a welcoming, safe, and civil workplace.

As discussed in other chapters in this book, a civil workplace makes for greater job satisfaction for employees. It is also linked to improved teamwork and a more positive environment overall. Knowing that civility in the workplace is best for everyone does not mean that conflicts will not arise, however. In addition to developing and enforcing civility policies, other suggestions include offering ongoing training, seeking feedback from employees on their perceptions of the workplace, and continuing to resolve any issues that arise.

When reviewing civility policies from educational institutions, you might assume that the focus would be on instructors and institutional staff leading the charge. In the case of San Jose Evergreen Community College District, the assumption would be incorrect. Its civility statement addresses students, employees, and trustees, with students first on the list. One of the areas in the statement that I found most appealing was under the heading of Guide Posts. The first item reads, "Civility begins with me." I see no better way of encouraging the growth of civility. If we are all charged with personally being responsible for civility, acting in a respectful manner and treating people with courtesy, then perhaps the rate of incivility will decline. Every person is responsible for his or her or their actions. No more anonymity and no more blaming others.

Diffusing the Uncivil Virtual Environment

The first rule of thumb in diffusing incivility in the virtual environment involves leadership. As mentioned previously in this book, organizations in which leaders display the behaviors desired of employees and embody the principles of respect and courtesy stand a greater chance of reducing incidences of incivility than do others. If individuals have a buy-in to decisions regarding the development of policies and procedures for managing civility, they are more likely to participate in all aspects of those policies.

In many cases, though, we are not discussing work-related incivility. We are talking day-to-day personal acts of individuals who post to social media networks and create intense levels of hostility and anger simply because they want to. These people have no punishment to fear that deters them from doing whatever they desire. For these situations, other users of these platforms have to take the responsibility for shutting down the discussions or at least keeping them from escalating. A trend is developing among platforms that are creating standards for participation and enforcing them as mechanisms for cutting off those who exhibit acts of incivility. However, more progress is needed in eliminating rude and inappropriate posts and online behaviors.

One suggestion for social networking companies would be to develop a training program to help users understand and identify acts of incivility before they engage in discussions in that environment. Providing definitions and explanations with examples of incivility in the social media environment could be extremely helpful to some, clarifying less understood types of incivility, such as challenging an expert by posting alternative information that is not based on fact. While most people would know what blatant incivility looks like—cursing, name-calling, and so on—the more subtle approaches can often go unnoticed and even trick users into participating in the discussions.

Addressing E-mail Incivility

An important point to consider regarding online communication, and I share this one with my students, never type a message (of any kind—e-mail, text, instant message) when you are angry. When you are angry, your message takes on a different tone, one of hostility and confrontation. If you are determined to type a message, use your word processing software to create a draft. You cannot send your message from that program, so you are safe. Once you have cooled down, then you can re-consider your message and how you wish to edit it or possibly delete it. You often will save yourself some trouble and avoid creating a hostile situation. Many times, our "off-the-cuff" thoughts that we include in our messages when we are frustrated or angry lead to the distribution of uncivil communications.

Dr. Susan Whitbourne raised the question of e-mail incivility in her article for *Psychology Today* when she asked if people even realized they were being rude in e-mails. She hypothesized that people assumed that matter-of-fact responses to e-mails (e.g., a comment or answer to a question) were not acts of rudeness or incivility. However, recipients of those types of messages disagreed. Since e-mail communication is one way, the recipient has no other contextual cues that a face-to-face response would provide. Whitbourne provided a couple of examples of statements in uncivil e-mails: "I couldn't be less confident in your ability, but here is the next set anyway" and "Try these next tasks, genius." She stated that those condescending or derisive statements could have been reworded into supportive messages that reflect a positive supervisory comment showing the employee's contributions are valued. Whitbourne suggested that when writing e-mail feedback, we should always turn criticisms into terms that cushion it with support. Start with the positive aspects (for a student, "you put a lot of work into this project"), then insert your criticisms but using a neutral and objective tone and words ("these are the areas or parts that require work"), and end on a positive note ("I look forward to seeing your next draft"). I, along with many other professors, recommend using a very similar approach to writing bad news messages in the business communication course. We teach students to start with a neutral buffer and follow that with explanations with the bad news embedded inside the explanations or reasons and end on a positive, forward-looking note. We remind students to avoid the use of negative words and to focus on the positives. Using this indirect approach keeps students, employees, customers, and clients from feeling bad and giving up or becoming defensive or combative.

The first step in the writing process is to make sure that the communication medium you have chosen is right for your message. Sometimes we default to e-mail because it is fast, and we can get our message out without delay. Nonetheless, we do face certain situations in which e-mail is not the most appropriate medium. A face-to-face meeting, a video chat, or a phone call may be a better choice. This decision is exceedingly true in the virtual environment as "words on a screen" can be misunderstood quite easily. If you examine the purpose behind your message and determine it to be something confidential or sensitive in nature, an e-mail is not your best choice. If you believe the recipient may have an emotional response to the message, pick something more personal than e-mail. When obtaining customers' or clients' reactions to an important idea, e-mail is not a good option. In any event, knowing the purpose of your message is vital to selecting the proper medium to convey it. You should not be a coward and hide behind electronic communication when the information you must convey is difficult or unpleasant (i.e., firing someone).

You will recall that incivility can be either active or passive. As I mentioned earlier, I have been guilty of passive incivility by not responding to e-mails in a timely fashion. Some of the messages I receive do not appear to require a response. Yet, I often get a follow-up message asking if I received the first message. One way to avoid this conundrum is to ask for a read receipt in your e-mail program when you are getting ready to send the message. Using this tool allows you, the sender, to be notified when the recipient opens and reads your message, thereby eliminating the need to contact that person to ask if the message was received. If you know that your message does not require any response, you can also include the phrase "No need to respond" at the end of it so that the recipient knows you are not anticipating any response. These little tips help to avoid any appearance of passive incivility.

One of the behaviors that irritates me the most is when a sender spells my name incorrectly in the e-mail or uses an incorrect courtesy title in the salutation. I suppose that may seem trite to some, but following the guidelines for professionalism dictates that the recipient's name should be spelled correctly with the proper courtesy title in place. Despite having my name in multiple places in my online classes, students still misspell it. They also address me with the courtesy title "Mrs." even though I hold a PhD. I have explained to them on numerous occasions about the importance of a person's name and using the correct form of address in communications; however, with each semester that passes, I see more of the same.

When students misspell my name, their e-mail messages often do not arrive in my inbox, leading to some follow-up communication that is accusatory and often hostile. They are unaware that they have misspelled my name in the e-mail address, and I have no exact explanation as to the reason for the missing e-mail as I cannot prove my name was misspelled, so they default to the belief that I am lying to them. Even after I attempt to smooth over the issue, whether by having them check their sent box to see how the e-mail was addressed or allowing them to re-submit an assignment or to have an extension on an assignment due date, I often can still detect the distrust in their voices when speaking with me.

The final step in drafting an e-mail message should always be to double-check the recipient's name and e-mail address. You should never press send until you have verified the information is correct, spelled correctly, and has no additional letters or reversed letters in it. Remember Dale Carnegie's quote about a person's name: "Remember that a person's name is to that person the sweetest and most important sound in any language."

As I stated in the preceding paragraphs, you also need to use a proper salutation for your e-mail message. When you are writing an e-mail in a professional setting, you need a salutation that includes a courtesy title and the last name of the individual to whom you are writing. Aside from professional courtesy titles such as Dr., Reverend, Rabbi, President, Senator, and so on, you also have Mr., Mrs., Ms., and Mx. The courtesy title Mx. was added to Emily Post's recently released centennial edition of *Etiquette* as a mechanism for addressing nongender identifying individuals, or individuals whose names do not readily identify their gender as they can be both male and female names (e.g., Kelly, Robin). A courtesy title is a form of respect and one that should be carefully considered when creating e-mails. Extreme caution also should be exercised in using the first name of the individual in your greeting unless your recipient is well known to you, and you have previously established a first-name basis relationship.

So, what can we do if we receive a rude e-mail from a customer or client or even a co-worker or student? We need to handle the situation with professionalism by taking the following into consideration:

- **The time of day**. If you reply to the e-mail late or early in the day, you could be escalating the incivility. If a co-worker receives a message at 6 a.m., that message could be perceived as rude.
- **The tone of your message**. Always aim for a positive tone. If you are unsure how your message reads, ask someone to read your response before you send it.
- **Restraint**. Include only the information needed. Do not embellish or add anything extra. Leave out any sarcasm or jokes, which may be misinterpreted or taken literally. Think how your message would be perceived if it were published on page 1 of a newspaper where everyone could read it.

- **Delay response**. Avoid sending an e-mail response when you are upset. Make every effort to be polite and professional regardless of how angry or offended you are.

An important point to remember about e-mail is that aside from being rude or disruptive, it can also be used as evidence if an organization is ever sued. Even though we are discussing civility and how to break the incivility hold on virtual environments, you also must keep in mind that what you write and share is open to legal scrutiny. Maintaining civility in your communication serves more than one purpose.

E-mails have long been a bone of contention, creating misunderstandings and requiring the need for follow-up messages to clarify points of communication. Adobe surveyed over 1,000 American workers to learn how much time on average they spend per day on e-mail. Findings from that study revealed that people spent more than five hours per day on e-mail. The number of hours involved in e-mail communication speaks to the various issues present in this environment. When you have no body language, eye contact, gestures, posture, vocalics, or other physical elements to use as complements to the words on the screen, you do not know exactly the meaning the writer or sender had for those words. Thus, we can easily understand how incivility can infiltrate e-mail. Nevertheless, you do not need to perpetuate the cycle of incivility by making your response in the heat of moment and adding fuel to the existing fire. When possible, reach out to the individual who wrote the heated message via another communication channel—preferably by phone or in person. Often when given the opportunity to fully explain the situation, people change their approach and de-escalate the rudeness inherent in the e-mail message.

For a quick checklist for ensuring civility in e-mail, go to the Checklists section of this book.

Addressing Social Media Incivility

As discussed previously, social media is a hotbed for acts of incivility. However, we do not have to engage in discussions where these types of interactions are occurring. As we learned, attempting to change some-one's perspective about religious beliefs or political leanings is an impos-sible task, especially if those individuals are receiving support via "likes" or "thumbs up" from other members of the social networking sites. You may contribute as many facts as you desire, but if the individual who is posting the comments continues to receive enough encouragement, that person will escalate the uncivil behavior into personal attacks against you and any others who support your posts.

Growing up in a small town in south Mississippi, I learned from my grandfather when I was very young that you cannot argue with a fence post. He used that analogy to help me understand that some people just like to argue, will not actively listen to any proven facts because they already have their minds made up, and will attack you verbally if you continue to press the point. I regularly see that occurring on social media networking sites. Some people just like to argue or to spread falsehoods or sensational half-truths. Those people connect with like-minded others and form their own communities, which is what social media network-ing sites were designed to do—help people form communities of like-minded individuals. The problem arises when people who do not believe the same, think the same, or engage in the same practices enter the com-munity. Losing control of the community to outsiders is unacceptable.

I have been on the receiving end of rude comments and personal attacks on social media sites. When I attempted to share information from a legitimate source that upended something an individual had posted as fact, I was immediately attacked as a "commie liberal" or worse. All that was needed was that one name-calling post, and suddenly, I was the brunt of every slur you can imagine, from "ignorant southerner" to some that I cannot include in this book because they refer to female body parts. Instead of responding in anger, I moved on. I knew that anything I posted would be seen as fodder for more cannon fire. One of my friends did respond on my behalf to defend me, and I reached out to her and thanked her for doing so, telling her that she did not need to worry about my reaction to the nasty posts.

The best approach to situations involving incivility in social media networking is to remain respectful. Always use appropriate language, never coarse, rough, or rude words. If you maintain proper grammar and spelling as well, you have an advantage. However, that also can be a double-edged sword as your writing style can be used against you in a derogatory fashion. You certainly have the right to disagree with people on social networking sites. However, you should always be respectful. People are entitled to their own opinions, and opinions vary from person to person. Keep in mind that you can offer a rebuttal to something that has been posted, but you must do so with facts, not personal opinions. Even then, your post may not be well received.

As with e-mail, any posts you make to social media networking sites should avoid using all capital letters so that no one thinks you are screaming or yelling (flaming). If you want to use emoticons to show meaning, do so. Emoticons can often help defray possible misinterpretations of written statements because they convey emotions. You can also use common acronyms (e.g., LOL for laugh out loud). If you prefer to show a state of mind when you are writing your post, you can include words in brackets beside the text (e.g., [grin]).

The best advice for interacting on social media networking sites is to be respectful and considerate. Attempt to engage with others, but when you find yourself in a situation where incivility is dominating the discussion, remember you have choices: stay and attempt to de-escalate the situation, or leave. The main goal, though, is to not get dragged into the incivility fray because you become angry and frustrated. Everything you write is visible for the world to see.

> To assist you with ensuring that you are practicing civility in your social media posts—and handling any negative comments you may find posted to your social media posts—see the Checklists in this book.

Addressing Online Learning, Training, and Meeting Incivility

So many things can go wrong in the online environment when you are attempting to teach, learn, train, meet, or present. One of the quickest ways to create a frustrating situation for participants is by being unfamiliar with the platform you are using to deliver or receive these sessions.

No one wants to hear that this session is the first time you have ever used XYZ program as the first thing out of your mouth. If you do so, you have set the stage for total disengagement of your participants. They have lost trust in you.

Prior to the COVID-19 pandemic, many people had limited experience with online meeting platforms. While they were in use in multiple organizations and institutions, they were not the norm. When businesses and schools were forced to close their physical locations in early 2020, online meeting platforms quickly escalated in use. However, virtual meeting etiquette and norms were unclear. People were unsure of how to handle themselves in these situations. Did they make eye contact? Where? Could they eat food while online? Did they need to dress professionally?

Individuals charged with teaching, training, hosting, or presenting had to acquire skills related to techniques and behaviors for the environment. First, they had to learn the platform. Being familiar with the operation of the platform was vital to the success of their program. They learned the importance of arriving early and performing a system check to ensure that everything was working properly. In addition, arriving early allowed the host to interact with participants who also arrived early and to help them get settled by answering any questions or assisting with any technical needs.

Hosts of these teaching, training, meeting, or presenting sessions found themselves devising plans for the sessions to help them stay on track and maintain momentum so that they could conclude on time. Dressing appropriately was important. Everyone knows what pajamas look like, and wearing a baseball cap because you did not want to comb your hair just creates a problem with eye contact.

One of the best rules of thumb for people who engage in these virtual sessions is to have an office specifically designated as your place of work, whether in your home or elsewhere. Stage your video area so that you have a clear workspace (no clutter on your desk). The use of a green screen (one that attaches to your desk chair is best) can also be of great benefit as it allows you to use a virtual background during your sessions so that your participants do not have a view of your office or any surroundings. Lighting is also important in these sessions. If possible, you should place your desk in a location where you are facing the sun. If you cannot do so, then a lamp or ring light would work.

Furthermore, the placement of your web camera is important. You want to make sure that your head is centered on the screen and that you are looking directly at the camera. The camera should not be below you and pointing up your nose or too high above you and looking down on the top of your head. If you have a limited number of participants (i.e., such as might occur in a meeting), you will want to have them introduce themselves. Give everyone a chance to say who they are and what they do. If your training session is small, then do the same there. Most often, classes have large numbers of students in them, so having them introduce themselves on camera would take a significant amount of class time. You can use other tools to have them perform that task after class ends.

The goal for these preparations is to project professionalism. You are establishing your credibility through these actions. One important point to remember is to avoid distractions. Whether you are the host or a participant, you should mute your mobile phone and your microphone when not speaking. Being credible with your participants goes a long way toward establishing a respectful environment.

Once you have handled the tasks of preparing for virtual teaching, training, meeting, or presenting, then you must consider how to handle potential conflict. Since you want your participants to be engaged in the session, you will be happy when they participate in discussions. However, you will find yourself on occasion having to facilitate a *hot moment*. The University of Michigan Center for Research on Teaching and Learning defines hot moment as that instance when a sudden eruption of conflict or tension occurs in the class. The hot moment definition can also be applied to training sessions, presentations, and meetings because any time you have people engaged in discussions, disagreements will occur. So, what can you do to facilitate those hot moments and keep them from deteriorating into shouting matches involving name-calling and abusive language?

- **Make sure you have set the stage for discussions**. You want to inform your learners, trainees, or participants what the rules are for a discussion. Explain why following the rules is important to maintaining civility.
- **When tensions arise, decide whether you need to address the issue immediately or take it up separately with**

individual participants. Some issues may require immediate attention and others can be delayed. However, you must guide your participants back to the topic at hand and away from any further escalation. Be cautious in your response so that you do not appear to take sides.

- **Remind participants of your discussion guidelines**. Just re-state the guidelines regarding incivility— for example, no personal attacks, openness to hearing others' perspectives, accountability for the effects of our words on others.

- **If possible, connect the hot moment to session topics or goals** (or course topics or goals). When participants are displaying such big emotions, what does that say about the topic you are covering? Can any course or session materials help inform or anchor the discussion that follows that hot moment?

- **Attempt to clarify participant comments**. If possible, try to help participants rephrase or explain their comments. Sometimes people will say insulting or marginalizing things when they are trying to understand something new or feeling that their personal views are being challenged. If you think that is the case, you can give the participant a chance to explain the thought process behind the remark (e.g., What do you mean by X? or I heard you saying Y; is that what you meant to say"?)

- **Try to depersonalize portions of the disagreement that have emerged among participants**. Instead of using "what X said versus what Y said," refer to "this disagreement about topic A" or "the use of phrase/word X in this context." By using these phrases, you are minimizing unproductive defensiveness while simultaneously inviting more participants into the discussion. You can also depersonalize the discussion by acknowledging when a widely held view has been raised: "Many people share this perspective. What might their reasons be?" Follow that up with, "And why might others object to or feel disrespected by this view?"

- **Ask for additional points of view**. You can say that "we have heard perspectives A and B," "how else might you think about this question?" to move the focus of the conversation away from individual speakers and onto the ideas or perspectives they were raising.

- **Assist the participants in finding common ground**. Help them identify a shared value (e.g., "I hear that you both care deeply about X, but you have strongly divergent ideas about how to achieve that"). You can also ask the other participants what common threads run through the two perspectives as well as how they differ.

- **Give participants the benefit of the doubt**. Occasionally people will speak words that seem to devalue other people or perspectives. So, while giving the benefit of the doubt as to their word choices, you can also explain the potential impact of given language choices (e.g., "I could easily imagine that your use of that metaphor would feel like an insult to classmates who . . .").

- **Use a three- to five-minute journaling exercise**. You can offer a prompt to your participants after discussing these intense issues that will allow them to reflect on the issues raised (e.g., "Hearing other participants' thoughts and perspectives in the session today provided me with an opportunity to _____.").

When you have a discussion in your virtual session that erupts into a hot moment, you need to take steps immediately to manage the situation. Once that session ends, though, you need to follow up with your students, trainees, or participants to gauge their experience with the session and to ensure that they did not feel targeted or personally affronted by whatever emerged.

Though not a virtual class, I had a similar experience with a hot moment during an onsite course. Students were engaged in a discussion focusing on events and event planning that escalated when a student veteran began disparaging Colin Kaepernick and his "taking a knee" protest during the national anthem. A couple of other students chimed in with statements of agreement, and before I could intervene, I noticed a student gathering her belongings getting ready to leave the class. I asked if she was leaving, and she said that she was because she could not participate in the discussion. I asked her to stay and share her thoughts so that we had balanced perspectives. She refused.

After class, I sent an e-mail to her in which I apologized for being unable to intervene quickly enough to defray the discussion to avoid the discomfort she experienced. Also, I reiterated the need for her to provide her perspective so that others in the class could hear both sides and encouraged her to speak out when she felt marginalized. She responded to my e-mail and thanked me for checking on her and for explaining the situation. She also stated that she felt she could not say anything because the other student was a veteran, and her response would have appeared to be anti-American. We followed up a few more times, and by the end of the course, she was speaking out more frequently and contributing to class discussions. She had to feel that her perspective was appreciated before doing so, though.

The foregoing example can apply to virtual classes as well. You must pay attention to the silent participants, the ones who go dark during a discussion and refuse to comment. They are the ones that can be most impacted by any element of incivility in the session. Their perceptions that no one wants to hear what they have to say or that no one will listen to them can prevent them from sharing thoughtful and thought-provoking ideas. If you have participants who are always talking, always answering questions, you may have to simply say that you would like to hear from others in the group. Without intervention, you may never know the effects of a discussion on some of your participants. Also, by participating in these uncomfortable discussions, your participants will learn to better manage conflict with their peers and supervisors in the workplace.

Make clear your expectations for civil behavior before a destructive situation occurs. This can be accomplished by inclusions in the employee handbook or as a posting in the online meeting/learning platform. For online classes offered via colleges and universities, one way to prevent acts of incivility is to include a list of the unacceptable behaviors in the course syllabus. As a further step, instructors can provide a description of each behavior and an explanation as to why it is unacceptable. The syllabus establishes a formal record of the unacceptable behaviors as well as the consequences of engaging in those uncivil acts.

As with any other venue, incivility in teaching and learning and meeting environments can take many forms. Therefore, no one approach will work for every situation. However, you should take the following steps for every incident:

- Remain calm and focused.
- Respond to the problem immediately.
- Stick to the consequences indicated in the handbook or syllabus.
- Administer the consequences for the uncivil behavior when warranted.

You cannot waver on the consequences or on administering the consequences for any uncivil behavior. To do so would damage your credibility. You must be consistent in your approach to the situation while maintaining your professionalism. Be polite, courteous, respectful, considerate, gracious, kind, and cordial. The culture of your online class or virtual group depends on consistency and adherence to the established standards.

For a quick checklist to ensure civility in your online classes, training sessions, meetings, and presentations, please refer to the Checklists section in this text.

Addressing Text Messaging Incivility

Texting has rapidly evolved into the most used communication tool. People use texts to set appointments, break up, fire employees, contact family, communicate with customers and clients, and any number of other purposes. What previously would have involved a phone call often is sent by text. And many of the interactions that should be handled in person are dealt with through texts. Professional text messages, much like e-mails, should adhere to the rules for grammar, spelling, and punctuation. You should not use all capital letters in text messages either, as that means you are shouting or yelling at the recipient. While texting is seen as a casual form of communication, many businesses now allow employees to text with customers and clients. In doing so, they are relying on their employees to follow professional guidelines for interacting with those individuals.

When texting with someone who does not have your phone number, you need to introduce yourself and explain where you are from, what organization or business. Keep your message brief. If you need to convey a lot of information, make a phone call, or send an e-mail instead. When you receive a text, you should respond as soon as possible. If you believe your response will be too lengthy for a reply, send a short reply indicating that you will send a more complete message via phone or e-mail.

Avoid using text speak or brief forms/abbreviations (e.g., IMHO, TTYL) in professional texts. Many people do not know the meanings of text speak and will be confused by your message. Also, when writing professional messages, regardless of the communication channel you use, you should always spell your words in full and not use acronyms.

While you may think this information does not appear to relate to incivility, the actions discussed before are all about respect and courtesy. Being respectful of people's time and courteous when considering your recipients' needs embody civility.

For a quick checklist on ensuring civility in your text messaging, please refer to the Checklists section in this book.

As the bulk of our communication is via text, e-mail, and other digital forms, the opportunity for misunderstanding increases. When misunderstanding arises, conflict follows. Because we spend so much time in the virtual environment, we can avoid conflict, or we can develop the online disinhibition effect. The online disinhibition effect leads us to react more aggressively and to respond in a heated communication without considering the potential consequences of our actions. Leaders of businesses, organizations, and institutions must model good behavior, what they want to see in their employees. I am reminded of the advice I read in a poem by Dorothy Nolte titled *Children Learn What They Live*. In the case of leaders, they can substitute the word "employees" in the place of children so that it reads in part, "If employees live with criticism, they learn to condemn. If employees live with hostility, they learn to fight." The same advice applies to managers, teachers, and trainers. Your behavior should set the pattern for others' behavior.

Leaders also need to stop making excuses for employees' rude behavior. When an employee reports that another employee is creating a problem, do not dismiss those concerns. Also, by addressing disrespectful behavior as soon as it happens, leaders are demonstrating that they will always hold everyone accountable. Failure to do so, encourages employees to continue conduct that causes pain or discomfort for others.

Organizations desiring to build a culture of civility can do so by deliberately hiring people who demonstrate good manners. This behavior is typically easy to assess during interviews. In addition, employers can use their personal network to locate information on job candidates. They may be able to find evidence of toxic behavior. Also, organizations can incorporate civility training into their employee development programs. Consistently reinforcing positive behavior is another way of building a culture of civility.

One of the biggest impacts on civility in any environment is that of examples set by high profile individuals. When public figures engage in rudeness on television, social media, or at public events, that behavior becomes normalized and accepted. Within a few months, that incivility will show up in online classes, training sessions, e-mails, texts, virtual meetings, and social media networking posts. While we cannot correct the behaviors of public figures, we can assist our learners, employees, and participants with navigating the pitfalls of an uncivil environment and help them to reassess their approach to communication. Having a plan in place, using civility training, and continually reinforcing and supporting the individuals involved in your classroom or workplace will only help to build a culture of civility in the long run. Once people learn that uncivil acts are unacceptable, that our culture was not built on the premise of rudeness and boorish behavior, then we stand a chance of rebuilding a civil society.

References

"Civility Statement." 2022-2023. San Jose Evergreen Community College District. 2019. https://catalog.evc.edu/college-profile/civility-statement/civility-statement.pdf (accessed August 10, 2019).

"Making the Most of Hot Moments in the Classroom." 2020. University of Michigan Center for Research on Learning and Teaching (CRLT), Fall. https://docs.google.com/document/d/1tuMuMVnI7soHLcTNxzCTqcpkun0ASHW_WvNuxphyyxA/edit.

"Policy 2.35 Civility In the Workplace." n.d. State of Virginia. Department of Human Resource Management, p. 7. www.dhrm.virginia.gov/docs/default-source/hrpolicy/policy-2-35-civility-in-the-workplace-policy.pdf.

Dale Carnegie Training. n.d. *Dale Tip #6: A Person's Name Is the Sweetest Sound.* https://dalecarnegieboston.tumblr.com/post/26913630460/dale-tip-6-a-persons-name-is-the-sweetest.

Galbraith, M.W. and M.S. Jones. 2010. "Understanding Incivility in Online Teaching." *Journal of Adult Education* 39, no. 2. https://files.eric.ed.gov/fulltext/EJ930240.pdf.

Gurchiek, K. February 12, 2019. "6 Tips for Responding to Rude E-mails: Rude E-mails Are Annoying and Can Bring the Workplace Down." *SHRM.* www.shrm.org/resourcesandtools/hr-topics/technology/pages/rude-e-mail.aspx.

Hess, A.J. September 22, 2019. "Here's How Many Hours American Workers Spend on E-mail Each Day." *NBC: Make It.* www.cnbc.com/2019/09/22/heres-how-many-hours-american-workers-spend-on-email-each-day.html.

Jayson, S. August 8, 2011. "At Work, No More Mr. Nice Guy." *USA Today.* Gale in Context: Opposing Viewpoints 01A. https://link.gale.com/apps/doc/A253951311/OVIC?u=tel_middleten&sid=ebsco&xid=5174f737 (accessed October 22, 2022).

Nolte, D.L. n.d. "Children Learn What They Live." *Poster.* www.etsy.com/listing/742023903/children-learn-what-they-live-poem-by.

Owens, D.M. February 2012. "Incivility Rising: Researchers Say Workers Might Not Have the Time to Be Civil." *HR Magazine*, p. 33.

Scarbrough, S.J. 2020. *Civility Rules*. ForbesBooks. ISBN: 9781930863401.

Whitbourne, S.K. September 14, 2013. "Are Your E-mails Unintentionally Rude?" *Psychology Today.* www.psychologytoday.com/ca/blog/fulfillment-at-any-age/201309/are-your-emails-unintentionally-rude.

Checklists

Ensuring Civility in E-mail

1.	Avoid writing and sending e-mail when angry, frustrated, or upset.
2.	Use a professional e-mail address.
3.	Use professional salutations with appropriate courtesy titles (Ms., Mr., or Mx.). Avoid the use of first names unless there is a clear friendly relationship already established.
4.	Include a clear subject line that explains the purpose of the message.
5.	Respond to e-mails in a timely fashion (within 24 hours) unless the message involves an emergency.
6.	Use a clear font and an easy-to-read type size (10 to 12 point).
7.	Adhere to all rules of grammar, spelling, and punctuation.
8.	Avoid using all capital letters that indicate shouting or yelling. If you need to emphasize information, use boldfacing, italicizing, or underlining.
9.	Avoid publicly criticizing people in business e-mail messages by using inappropriate language and being hostile, blunt, rude, or obscene.
10.	Avoid sarcasm.
11.	Use exclamation points sparingly or not at all.
12.	Spell out acronyms the first time you use them.
13.	Keep e-mails to one screen (be concise and clear).
14.	Include a signature block on your e-mails.
15.	Proofread your e-mail before you send it.
16.	Double-check the recipient's name and e-mail address to ensure correctness before sending.

Ensuring Civility in Instant Messaging

1.	Make sure instant messaging is the right communication tool for the situation. Use instant messaging only when it is the most appropriate choice.
2.	Refrain from messaging someone when that person is marked as unavailable or if you have received an away message.
3.	When responding to someone's message, type your answer, send it, and then wait for the recipient's reply before sending another message.
4.	Use a polite, friendly tone.
5.	Write short messages. Respect your recipient's time.
6.	Start your message with a greeting (e.g., Hello) and mention your recipient's name.
7.	Write clear messages with enough detail to ensure understanding of the message.
8.	Do not use instant messaging to deliver bad news.
9.	Follow all grammar, spelling, and punctuation rules.
10.	Adhere to number rules.
11.	Do not use all capital letters in any single word or sentence.
12.	Avoid using any brief forms (e.g., GR8, ROFL) because they are perceived as unprofessional and can lead to misunderstandings.
13.	Avoid acronyms unless your recipient is familiar with them.
14.	Avoid using technical jargon unless your reader is familiar with it.
15.	Avoid using slang or colloquial expressions as they can cause confusion or misunderstandings.
16.	Avoid using abbreviations because they can cause confusion and misunderstandings.
17.	Avoid using emoticons unless your company has a policy that allows for the use of them. Emoticons are generally considered unprofessional in business writing.
18.	Use humor cautiously as your message can be misinterpreted.
19.	Avoid letting a message thread continue for too long. Know when to stop.
20.	Indicate that you are signing off ("got to go," or "bye") and then type your name at the end of the instant message.
21.	Proofread, edit, and revise your instant messages before you send them.
22.	Log off instant messaging when you are not using it.
23.	Be wary of having more than one messaging thread running at a time.

Ensuring Civility in Social Media

1.	Be accountable.
2.	Create a professional online reputation.
3.	Be polite and respectful.
4.	Do not discuss your employer or co-workers.
5.	Do not post anything that you would not want employers, current clients, or future clients to see.
6.	Never post when you are jet-lagged, intoxicated, angry, or upset.
7.	Use proper grammar, spelling, and punctuation in your posts.

Handling Negative Social Media Comments	
1.	Do not ignore customer or client comments. OR Ignore them and hope they go away. They may, but if they do, your business could lose them as a customer or client, and they will tell others about their negative experience with your company or you.
2.	Delete them and get the same results as ignoring them.
3.	Do not respond with an angry or defensive post. If you do, you will make a major public relations error.
4.	Attempt to smooth things over with an apology. Offering an apology is better than ignoring them or deleting them, but if you do not provide a solution with your apology, your words will not ring true.
5.	Respond quickly and acknowledge the comment. Most customers posting a complaint on social media expect your response within 60 minutes. If you cannot provide an explanation or a full response within that time, simply thank them and acknowledge that you read the post and will reply more fully by a given date and time.
6.	Take time to calm down before responding. If a customer's post angers you or puts you on the defensive, you want to take some time before responding to avoid making any damaging or inflammatory remarks.

Ensuring Civility in Text Messaging

1.	Make sure that the person you are texting is receptive to texting. Some people prefer a phone call or e-mail.
2.	Avoid sending text messages concerning important, complex, or controversial business matters. You should select a more formal communication channel for these.
3.	Reserve text messaging for reasonable times and be sensitive to time zone differences when texting international business contacts.
4.	Avoid including any confidential information in a text message.
5.	Avoid discussing any legal matters via text message.
6.	Be courteous in your messages.
7.	Avoid texting too frequently as that behavior can be seen as annoying or even potential harassment.
8.	Practice patience when awaiting a response to a text message, and avoid being a text nag by re-sending a text when you think too much time has elapsed. Call the individual instead.
9.	Avoid sending bad news via a text message. A face-to-face meeting is likely needed for this purpose.
10.	Write clear, succinct messages but include enough detail to ensure your recipient understands the purpose of your text message.
11.	Avoid using abbreviations or brief words/shorthand, as doing so is considered unprofessional and can easily create misunderstandings.
12.	Follow the rules of grammar, spelling, and punctuation in your text messages.
13.	Avoid typing in all capital letters, as that implies shouting or yelling.
14.	Before sending a text message, proofread to ensure that the autocorrect feature on your phone has not changed some of your words.
15.	Edit and revise your text messages before sending them.

Ensuring Civility in Online Classes, Training Sessions, Meetings, and Presentations

1.	Be prepared. Know your platform and the tools that you are using (e.g., chat rooms, whiteboard, polling, and so on).
2.	Establish a specific location for your virtual office where your computer and web camera can be positioned correctly and where you will have no interruptions.
3.	Use a green screen for your background so that you can project a virtual image of an office or other professional location. You avoid having participants see the walls and contents of your office or apartment by using a green screen.
4.	Dress appropriately. Be professional in appearance, using the same attention to detail you would if you were in a face-to-face setting.
5.	Arrive a few minutes early for your session so that you can test your technology to make sure everything is working properly (e.g., web camera, microphone, etc.). You should also interact with any participants that have arrived early to the session.
6.	Begin on time. If you are leading a virtual meeting, try to distribute an agenda for the meeting at least a week before the meeting date and time so that participants know the starting time and the topics to be covered.
7.	Maintain a good posture and eye contact (the web camera is your audience, not the monitor or computer screen).
8.	Explain the process for discussion and what constitutes incivility in that regard. Also provide details of how any acts of incivility will be addressed.
9.	Involve participants in the discussion. Avoid being a "talking head."
10.	If a hot moment arises during a discussion, handle it appropriately by defusing the situation.
11.	Do not allow yourself to become frustrated or angry at the incivility arising out of the discussion. Do not respond in anger.
12.	Use nonverbal communication to complement your words when possible; however, be mindful of vocal inflections that indicate sarcasm.
13.	Build in multiple forms of interaction and participation. Invite participation as often as possible by using polling, question and answer, or other tools in your online platform toolbox.
14.	Speak slowly and at the proper volume. Ask participants if you are speaking loudly enough.
15.	Create learning and listening conditions that allow sufficient opportunity for participants to absorb the information and consider its meaning. Use a "less is more" approach to preparing materials.
16.	Always end your online class, training session, meeting, or presentation on time. Plan for the time you are allotted and use it wisely. Do not go over.

About the Author

Dr. K. Virginia Hemby is a professor in the marketing department at Middle Tennessee State University. She earned a PhD in Adult Education with a concentration in Business Education from The University of Southern Mississippi. Dr. Hemby was the 2018 recipient of the John Robert Gregg Award, presented in recognition of dedication and outstanding contribution to business teachers and the profession of Business Education. She teaches undergraduate online Business Communication courses designed to assist students in acquiring skills in professional workplace writing and communicating.

Index

OTHER TITLES IN THE CORPORATE COMMUNICATION COLLECTION

Debbie DuFrene, Stephen F. Austin State University, Editor

- *Win Business with Relationships* by May Hongmei Gao
- *Technical Marketing Communication, Second Edition* by Emil B. Towner and Heidi L. Everett
- *The Thong Principle* by Donalee Moulton
- *How to Become a Master of Persuasion* by Tony Treacy
- *101 Tips for Improving Your Business Communication* by Edward Barr
- *Business Writing For Innovators and Change-Makers* by Dawn Henwood
- *Delivering Effective Virtual Presentations* by K. Virginia Hemby
- *New Insights into Prognostic Data Analytics in Corporate Communication* by Pragyan Rath and Kumari Shalini
- *Leadership Through A Screen* by Joseph Brady and Garry Prentice
- *Managerial Communication for Professional Development* by Reginald L. Bell and Jeanette S. Martin
- *Managerial Communication for Organizational Development* by Reginald L. Bell and Jeanette S. Martin
- *Business Report Guides* by Dorinda Clippinger
- *Strategic Thinking and Writing* by Michael Edmondson

Concise and Applied Business Books

The Collection listed above is one of 30 business subject collections that Business Expert Press has grown to make BEP a premiere publisher of print and digital books. Our concise and applied books are for...

- Professionals and Practitioners
- Faculty who adopt our books for courses
- Librarians who know that BEP's Digital Libraries are a unique way to offer students ebooks to download, not restricted with any digital rights management
- Executive Training Course Leaders
- Business Seminar Organizers

Business Expert Press books are for anyone who needs to dig deeper on business ideas, goals, and solutions to everyday problems. Whether one print book, one ebook, or buying a digital library of 110 ebooks, we remain the affordable and smart way to be business smart. For more information, please visit www.businessexpertpress.com, or contact sales@businessexpertpress.com.

www.ingramcontent.com/pod-product-compliance
Lightning Source LLC
Chambersburg PA
CBHW061336220326
41599CB00026B/5208